Dec, 1998

For Robert:

With kindest personal regards and deep gratitude for everything you have done for me — to keep me going!

Sincerely,
David Noel

PSALM 119
THE EXALTATION OF TORAH

BIBLICAL AND JUDAIC STUDIES FROM THE UNIVERSITY OF CALIFORNIA, SAN DIEGO

Volume 6

edited by
William Henry Propp

Previously published in the series:

1. *The Hebrew Bible and Its Interpreters*, edited by William Henry Propp, Baruch Halpern, and David Noel Freedman (1990).
2. *Studies in Hebrew and Aramaic Orthography*, by David Noel Freedman, A. Dean Forbes, and Francis I. Andersen (1992).
3. *Isaiah 46, 47, and 48: A New Literary-Critical Reading*, by Chris Franke (1994).
4. *The Book around Immanuel: Style and Structure in Isaiah 2–12*, by Andrew H. Bartelt (1996).
5. *The Structure of Psalms 93–100*, by David M. Howard Jr. (1997).

PSALM 119

THE EXALTATION OF TORAH

by

David Noel Freedman

David Noel Freedman

EISENBRAUNS
Winona Lake, Indiana
1999

Published for Biblical and Judaic Studies
The University of California, San Diego,
by
Eisenbrauns
Winona Lake, Indiana

Cataloging in Publication Data

Freedman, David Noel, 1922–
Psalm 119 : the exaltation of Torah / by David Noel Freedman
p. cm. — (Biblical and Judaic Studies from the University of California, San Diego ; v. 6)
Includes bibliographical references.
ISBN 1-57506-038-8 (alk. paper)
1. Bible. O.T. Psalm CXIX—Language, style. 2. Acrostics in the Bible. 3. Bible. O.T. Psalm CXIX—Relation to Pentateuch. 4. Bible. O.T. Pentateuch—Relation to Psalm CXIX. I. Title. II. Biblical and Judaic Studies ; v. 6.
BS1450 119th F74 1999
223′.206—dc21

99-046630
CIP

The paper used in this publication meets the minimum requirements of the American National Standard for Information Sciences—Permanence of Paper for Printed Library Materials, ANSI Z39.48-1984.⊗™

Contents

Preface

The alphabetic acrostic is one of the most easily identifiable poetic forms in the Hebrew Bible. Examples can be found in prophetic discourse (Nahum), the lament over the destruction of Jerusalem (Lamentations), liturgical song (Psalms), and wisdom literature (Proverbs). Yet its very obviousness has tended to deflect deeper exploration of its structure and purpose. Since Mowinckel denigrated the acrostics in the Psalms as a "disintegration of style," too often scholars have simply noted and then ignored the form.

There is no a priori reason that alphabetic acrostics should be less creative, expressive, or complex than other psalms. Thus the essays collected here investigate the acrostic format as a legitimate option for Israelite poets rather than as the refuge of uninspired epigones. In particular, these essays focus on the technical aspects of the psalms—metrics, syllable counts, colon length, and symmetry within and between the psalms—because such study provides the foundation for further consideration of the psalms' theology and poetics. The results show how the poets' creativity functions at all levels, from the individual line to the complete psalm and even to the entire alphabetic acrostic corpus.

There is as yet no consensus on biblical poetics, and some scholars may reject the data presented here as irrelevant or insignificant. This would be a mistake. The fruit of over twenty years' close reading of these psalms, the following essays reveal the poets' consummate mastery of the demanding acrostic form and deserve incorporation in future discussions of biblical poetic art.

Chapter 1
Alphabetic Acrostic Psalms

David Noel Freedman
and
Jeffrey C. Geoghegan

The book of Psalms is the principal repository of alphabetic acrostic poems in the Hebrew Bible, containing eight examples of this type. Other examples occur elsewhere, chiefly in Lamentations (four in the first four chapters of the book) but also in Proverbs (at the end) and in the original Hebrew of Ecclesiasticus or Ben Sira. The antitype (nonalphabetic but exhibiting the same formal or metrical structure) is even more widespread, being found in the Psalter, Proverbs, Job, and elsewhere, as well as in Lamentations (chap. 5).

The purpose of the present paper is to describe the group of alphabetic poems in the Psalter, to examine similarities and differences, and then to show how they form and fit into a larger symmetrical picture. The psalms under consideration in this paper are as follows: Psalms 9/10, 25, 34, 37, 111, 112, 119, and 145. While in the Hebrew Bible the first of these psalms has been divided into separate numbers, the poem is a single work, as the alphabetic pattern clearly shows, and this fact is reflected in the LXX, which presents the whole poem as a single composition, Psalm 9 according to its system of counting. Just why and how the psalm was divided in the MT is uncertain, but the fact that in the MT Psalm 10 has no separate heading implies that the division was artificial and occurred after an earlier edition (in which the Psalm was undivided) had appeared. The conclusion that the LXX preserves the earlier stage in the history of publication and transmission seems certain. We will therefore treat Psalms 9/10 as a single composition.

The number *eight* has an important place in biblical numerology, as we have tried to show on other occasions, especially in regard to these alphabetic acrostic poems.[1] The longest and most elaborate of all of the poems is in this

1. As we attempt to show here and in the two chapters on Psalm 119 below.

collection, Psalm 119, with its 8-line stanzas and repetition of the key letter in each of the 8 lines. The only comparable poem in the Hebrew Bible is the third chapter of Lamentations, in which the same pattern occurs, except that this poem is restricted to 3-line stanzas.[2] The number *eight* also figures in the traditional counting of the prophetic corpus, in which the four Former Prophets are matched by the four Latter Prophets (Joshua, Judges, Samuel, and Kings correspond to Isaiah, Jeremiah, Ezekiel, and the Book of the Twelve). The artificial character of the pattern is to be noted, as well as the dissolution of the symmetry in the Greek Bible, in which the system breaks down—with the inclusion of a book like Ruth in the first part and with the redivision of Samuel and Kings into four books, while in the second part the minor prophets were probably considered separate entries and not individual parts of a single, large entry. The placement of the book of Daniel among the prophets would likewise disrupt the other pattern, but the Hebrew Bible here preserves an original and intentional symmetry.

So beginning with the number *eight* we find, not surprisingly, that the psalms in question are clustered in two groups of four: four in the first book of the Psalms and four in the last book. Closer examination reveals a further division into pairs, a pattern reflective of a similar clustering of the masculine and feminine singular and plural key-word nouns in the Great Psalm (119 in the Hebrew text) itself. The pairs in the Psalter can be identified as follows:

I.	Psalms 9/10	//	Psalm 37
	Psalm 25	//	Psalm 34
II.	Psalm 111	//	Psalm 112

In each pair we find the same basic structure. Thus, in descending order: Psalms 9/10 and 37 have 2-line alphabetic units, while Psalms 25 and 34 have 1-line units, and Psalms 111 and 112 have half-line alphabetic units. Or, if we use the colon as the basic building block, then Psalms 111 and 112 have a single colon for each letter of the alphabet, while Psalms 25 and 34 have a bicolon for each letter, and Psalms 9/10 and 37 have a tetracolon (4 cola) with each letter. The sequence seems deliberate: the pairs are different from each other but at the same time are clearly related in a single arithmetic/geometric progression: 1 and 1, 2 and 2, 4 and 4. Hence $1 + 1 = 2$, $2 + 2$ or $2 \times 2 = 4$. If we go one step further, we come to $4 \times 4 = 16$, which is also the number of cola in each stanza of the Great Psalm 119, which is consequently placed after the preceding six psalms. We can set the equation up in tabular form as follows:

2. Lamentations 1 and 2 have the same overall structure, but the key letter appears only at the beginning of the first line of each stanza.

	Lines	*Cola*	*Totals*
Psalms 9/10	2	4	44 × 2 = 88
Psalm 25	1	2	22 × 2 = 44
Psalm 34	1	2	22 × 2 = 44
Psalm 37	2	4	44 × 2 = 88
Psalm 111	1/2	1	11 × 2 = 22
Psalm 112	1/2	1	11 × 2 = 22
	7	14	154 × 2 = 308
Psalm 119	8	16	176 × 2 = 352

While the first six psalms in their enumeration lead geometrically to Psalm 119, there remains a slight discrepancy in the numerical balance. The difference is made up in the last of the eight psalms, Psalm 145, which is similar to Psalms 25 and 34 in having 1-line, 2-colon alphabetic units. Thus the total number of lines or cola for the seven shorter psalms matches that of the Great Psalm. It would be difficult to suppose that any of this arrangement and organization could have happened by accident or random selection.

As often, if not always, in the symmetrical patterns of calculations of the biblical writers and especially the editors, there are significant deviations from the established norm. Therefore only the Great Psalm and the two shortest Psalms, 111 and 112, have every letter of the alphabet in place and order, and they alone keep the prescribed number of lines for each letter of the alphabet. All of the others omit certain letters and vary the units of cola or lines per letter as well as indulging or engaging in rearrangement and reordering of different kinds. The question always is: how much of the disorder is owing to deliberate manipulation to serve ends or purposes not always or immediately clear and how much is owing to inadvertent miscopying by a scribe or misinterpreting or misunderstanding on the part of later compilers and editors? Many scholars have believed that most of the deviations are due to scribal error or editorial misinterpretation, while a few may be deliberate deviations on the part of authors. Our judgment, after careful study both of the text and other scholarly corrections, is that many more of the variations are deliberate than scholars generally allow and that we have insufficiently appreciated either the subtle maneuvers in which the authors engaged or the degree to which they worked to avoid mere monotonous repetitions. As we proceed with an examination of the particular psalms, we will try to clarify and explain the discrepancies and deviations and just how and why they came about.

Psalms 111 and 112

We begin with the simplest pair, Psalms 111 and 112, which are twins and mirror images in all possible ways. They both follow the Hebrew alphabet in the same order, and they both consist of single cola, one per letter. Furthermore, they are the only two poems in the whole Hebrew Bible having this particular structure. Both have the same distinctive heading, shared with several others in this group from no. 111 through 117—a group of seven psalms, each of which begins or ends with the expression *hallĕlû yāh*: nos. 111 and 112 have the declaration as a heading; Psalm 113 in the MT has the same expression at the beginning and end of the psalm, as a result leaving Psalm 114 without the phrase at either end; Psalms 115, 116, and 117 all have the expression at the end. So the phrase appears seven times in this group of seven poems, but they are distributed in the MT so that the phrase appears as a heading in the first three psalms and as a closing in the last three. There is some variation in the way the middle expression is interpreted: in the MT it closes Psalm 113, whereas in the LXX it serves as the heading of Psalm 114, perhaps more in keeping with the general design of this group of psalms.

With respect to Psalms 111 and 112, the heading is precisely that—a heading—and outside of the alphabetic acrostic pattern. Nevertheless, the words may be part of the metrical pattern and not simply a heading or title for the psalm. A look at the parallel columns, listing the syllables per colon, shows that colon length varies within and between the poems, and few if any of the same lines in the two poems are identical in length. The range is from 5 to 9 or 10 syllables, and both mean and average are between 7 and 8. In spite of this lack of uniformity in the treatment of cola, characteristic of practically all Biblical Hebrew poetry, the total length of each poem is the same—identical in fact—remarkable and important, a widespread phenomenon.

Having two such psalms with the same gross structure is a distinct benefit in determining which features are regular or repeated and which are less rigidly controlled and subject to variation. The poems have much in common but are not the same. Some lines are duplicated (e.g., 111 [*waw*] and 112 [*waw*] and also 112 [*ṣadeh*]), which is identical except for the omission of initial *waw*); others are echoed. They may have been composed by the same author, or different authors may have worked within the common constraints. When it comes to meter or quantity, the structure is controlled formally by the alphabetic factor. The standard 22-letter alphabet in its traditional order is maintained throughout, and each letter is represented by a single colon. Variation occurs only in regard to the number of syllables and the number of accents. With respect to the latter, the dominant number is 3, as expected. Hence in each poem 14 of the 22 cola have 3 accents, but the other 8 depart from this norm: Psalm 111 divides the remaining 8 cola evenly between 2 and 4 accents (4 of each), thereby producing a symmetrical overall structure, as shown in the table. Accordingly the total of 66 accents for the whole poem conforms to the expected norm of 3 accents per colon: 22 × 3 = 66. We think it would serve no useful purpose to adjust the accents of the text to produce a uniform count of 3 accents per colon throughout the poem in the interest of perfect regularity of repetition. We should recognize that these relatively minor variations fall within the guidelines for such poetry, and the poet was free to stray modestly or moderately from the established norms.

In the case of Psalm 112, there is somewhat greater deviation on the part of the poet, especially when it comes to balancing 2- and 4-accent cola. In this psalm the 2s and 4s do not match up, since there is a preponderance of 4-accent cola in comparison with 2-accent cola (6:2 rather than 4:4, as in Psalm 112). How serious or significant this divergence is from a perceived norm (Psalm 111) may be beyond determination, in particular because we cannot be sure about how accents were assigned or distributed at the time of composition and to what extent poets themselves adhered to or departed from standard practice. We are largely dependent on Masoretic vocalization and accentuation, and it is not always a reliable guide. So we must acknowledge that counting accents is not a precise or decisive method for determining quantity in Hebrew poetry. In this instance, we note that one of the two psalms is slightly more regular than the other and can serve as the standard, while the other reflects a further range of variation from the presumed norm (see table 1).

The situation is similar in regard to syllable counting. Once again, there is a clustering around a presumed norm, namely 8 syllables per colon, but there is also a range of variation from a minimum of 6 syllables to a maximum of 9 in both poems. While the lowest number, 6, is represented by only one example in each poem and may therefore be regarded as unusual or even aberrant, the other three numbers are all well represented, and it would be a mistake to try to make the numbers under or over the norm conform to it. In fact, taking the poems together, 7-syllable cola are almost as numerous as 8-syllable cola (16 with 7 syllables, against 18 with 8 syllables, while 9 syllables occur in 8 cola) and actually outnumber the 8 in Psalm 112 (9 to 7, whereas in Psalm 111, 8 outnumbers 7 by 11 to 7). So we must reckon not only with a range but with an almost equal occurrence or distribution of 7- and 8-syllable cola. As with accents, so with syllables: flexibility and variation within overall limits were not only accepted and expected but probably encouraged to avoid excessive repetition and the resulting monotony or boredom. We note too that

Table 1. Accent Counts for Psalms 111 and 112

	111			112		111			112
(1)	3	א	(1)	3	(6)	4	כ	(6)	3
	3	ב		3		4	ל		4
Total	6		Total	6	Total	8		Total	7
(2)	3	ג	(2)	4	(7)	4	מ	(7)	4
	2	ד		3		2	נ		3
Total	5		Total	7	Total	6		Total	7
(3)	2	ה	(3)	2	(8)	3	ס	(8)	4
	3	ו		3		3	ע		3
Total	5		Total	5	Total	6		Total	7
(4)	3	ז	(4)	4	(9)	3	פ	(9)	3
	3	ח		3		2	צ		3
Total	6		Total	7		3	ק		3
					Total	8		Total	9
(5)	3	ט	(5)	4	(10)	4	ר	(10)	3
	3	י		2		3	ש		3
Total	6		Total	6		3	ת		3
					Total	10		Total	9

Total Accent Counts	
Psalm 111	Psalm 112
66	70

Psalm 112 has more variations and exhibits slightly greater flexibility in its particulars and details than Psalm 111, thereby showing perhaps that Psalm 111 serves as the standard, while Psalm 112 illustrates greater freedom and flexibility, a circumstance we will observe in the remaining pairs of alphabetic psalms. Most striking is the fact that, in spite of flexibility and variation in colon-length, the total number of syllables in both psalms is exactly the same. This time we come up with a total of 170, compared with 169 in an earlier

Table 2. Syllable Counts for Psalms 111 and 112

111			112	
(1)	8	א	(1)	9
	8	ב		8
Total	16		Total	17
(2)	7	ג	(2)	8
	9	ד		7
Total	16		Total	15
(3)	6	ה	(3)	6
	8	ו		8
Total	14		Total	14
(4)	8	ז	(4)	9
	7	ח		8
Total	15		Total	17
(5)	7	ט	(5)	7
	8	י		9
Total	15		Total	16

111			112	
(6)	8	כ	(6)	7
	8	ל		8
Total	16		Total	15
(7)	9	מ	(7)	9
	7	נ		9
Total	16		Total	18
(8)	8	ס	(8)	7
	9	ע		8
Total	17		Total	15
(9)	7	פ	(9)	8
	8	צ		7
	7	ק		7
Total	22		Total	22
(10)	8	ר	(10)	7
	7	ש		7
	8	ת		7
Total	23		Total	21

Total Syllable Counts	
Psalm 111	Psalm 112
170	170

count.[3] There are several minor differences between the two countings, but none of them is significant, and the difference is only due to the problem of how to count the syllables in a single word in each poem: *ḥepṣêhem* in 111 (ד) and *ʾašrê* in 112 (א). In the MT the count is 3 and 2 respectively, whereas

3. David Noel Freedman, "Acrostics and Metrics in Hebrew Poetry," *HTR* 65 (1972) 367–92.

there is reason to think that in classical times each had an added syllable. The difference is negligible in the overall count and, if we treat the two words in the same way, then the total for each poem will also be the same, whether 170 or 169 syllables[4] (see table 2).

The inference we draw is that the real concern was to make totals come out the same, while line lengths themselves could vary within relatively narrow limits. Practically every line in both poems falls within 1 syllable of the norm: 7–9. Only 1 line in each poem is at a larger degree of separation. This is a high degree of uniformity in itself, made even greater by the care taken to equate the totals. Given the flexibility at the level of the colon or half-line, the equality of the totals could hardly be the result of chance. Random selection might produce convergence once in awhile but not regularly or systematically. It is much more likely that the regular recurrence of equal totals (as also seen in Lamentations 1–3) is the result of careful planning and arranging on the part of the poet. The point is that in Hebrew poetry unlike, say, English poetry, the totals are not dictated by line length and meter. Shakespearean sonnets, for example, have about 140 syllables because they are defined by the number of lines (14) and the number of feet per line (iambic pentameter = 10). To get the same totals in Hebrew poetry requires diligent attention to overall planning and selection, since random choice will rarely if ever produce identical totals.

Psalms 25 and 34

The next pair of Psalms to be considered consists of Psalms 25 and 34. Since these have been studied in some detail elsewhere, we will only summarize the essential or relevant points here.[5] These psalms belong to the largest single subcategory of alphabetic acrostic poems in the Bible, in which the basic unit is the line or bicolon. Thus, in our group of eight psalms, Psalm 145 has this configuration. Proverbs 31 also belongs to this group. In addition there is a goodly number of nonalphabetic poems with the same overall structure, 1-line bicola, and generally of the 16-syllable, 6-accent variety as well (e.g., Proverbs 2, Lamentations 5, Psalm 33, etc.).

4. To the 170 total for each poem we should probably add the 4 syllables of the heading *hallĕlû-yāh*, since the latter, while occurring outside of the alphabetic structure, is not like most of the others, providing information about the psalm to follow but remaining an intrinsic part of the poem, a part that was sung or chanted in order to introduce the body of the work. This would give us a total of 174 syllables for each poem, very close to the expected norm of 176 syllables for such acrostic poems.

5. Cf. David Noel Freedman, "Patterns in Psalms 25 and 34," in *Priests, Prophets and Scribes: Essays on the Formation and Heritage of Second Temple Judaism in Honour of Joseph Blenkinsopp* (Sheffield: JSOT Press, 1992) 125–38.

What sets Psalms 25 and 34 apart and demonstrates that they form a distinctive, in fact unique, pair (not only in the Psalter but the whole Hebrew Bible), are the deliberate deviations from the established overall patterns. Both psalms omit the *waw* line or bicolon, and both psalms add a second *peh* line after the *taw* line that normally would end the poem. No other psalm or poem in the Hebrew Bible includes either of these features. Thus, as also is the case with Psalms 111 and 112, we have here a unique pair, a matching set.

It remains to examine the structure of both psalms in more detail and to see to what extent they match up or diverge from each other. On the basis of previous experience, specifically with respect to Psalms 111 and 112, we would expect overall symmetry and equality (in numbers and syllable-counting) and at the same time some significant deviations, since different strategies or tactics are used in coping with challenges and opportunities in versification. Table 3 provides the essential quantitative data.

On the basis of the tables and totals, we note that Psalm 25 will establish the norm or basic pattern for this pair. In this poem we count 20 bicola and 2 tricola (the *he*ʾ line and the *ḥet* line), making a total of 46 cola for the poem. While there are only the standard 22 lines in the poem (the omission of the *waw* line is made up for by the addition of the second *peh* line), the two tricola in effect give us an additional line, showing that the poet intended to write an augmented or enhanced alphabetic acrostic to incorporate added ornamentation and elaboration. Therefore, with the equivalent of 23 lines (note that the added cola both occur in the first half of the poem to make up for the loss of the *waw* line), there is not only an opening and a closing line but also a middle line, the 12th or the *lamed* line. Then, as already pointed out by others, if we take the first letters of the first, middle, and last lines of the poem we get the word *ʾlp*, which spells the Hebrew equivalent of our word *alphabet* (itself derived from the first two letters of the Phoenician-Hebrew, Greek-Latin alphabets).[6] In the case of Psalm 34, the enhancement is also present, but the poem is built up in a different manner. Instead of added cola, as in the case of Psalm 25, there are added words producing longer lines, not more of them. The end result is much the same, but the procedure is different and the superficial appearance quite different. These deviations and differences, however, are subsumed under an overall equality and

6. It is a curious and perhaps relevant fact that the two special letters in these poems, *waw* and *peh*, form an example of athbash (*ʾatbaš*), since *waw* is the sixth letter in the standard Hebrew alphabet, and *peh* is the sixth letter from the end. In effect the lost *waw* line is replaced by the added *peh* line. If the connection is deliberate, then the explanation may proceed from the addition of the second *peh* for the reason given in the text, to the elimination of the *waw* line to balance out the addition of the *peh* line, and then to the addition of two cola in lines near the missing *waw* line to fill out the first half of the poem to preserve and enhance its quantitative symmetry with the second half.

Table 3. Syllable Counts for Psalms 25 and 34

		25 Low	25 High			34 Low	34 High
א	(1)	4	5	א	(2)	10	10
		7	7			8	8
	Total	11	12		Total	18	18
ב	(2)	8	9	ב	(3)	8	8
		8	8			10	10
	Total	16	17		Total	18	18
ג	(3)	8	9	ג	(4)	8	8
		9	9			9	9
	Total	17	18		Total	17	17
ד	(4)	9	10	ד	(5)	10	10
		8	9			11	11
	Total	17	19		Total	21	21
ה	(5)	13	14	ה	(6)	9	9
		8	8			8	8
[ו]		8	9				
	Total	29	31		Total	17	17
ז	(6)	11	13	ז	(7)	10	10
		6	6			9	9
	Total	17	19		Total	19	19
ח	(7)	13	13	ח	(8)	6	6
		8	8			11	11
		6	7				
	Total	27	29		Total	17	17
ט	(8)	6	6	ט	(9)	10	10
		9	9			7	7
	Total	15	15		Total	17	17
י	(9)	8	8	י	(10)	9	9
		9	9			8	8
	Total	17	17		Total	17	17
כ	(10)	9	9	כ	(11)	9	9
		11	11			12	12
	Total	20	20		Total	21	21
ל	(11)	6	7	ל	(12)	7	7
		10	11			8	8
	Total	16	18		Total	15	15

		25 Low	25 High			34 Low	34 High
מ	(12)	8	8	מ	(13)	8	8
		7	7			8	8
	Total	15	15		Total	16	16
נ	(13)	6	6	נ	(14)	7	8
		6	6			9	10
	Total	12	12		Total	16	18
ס	(14)	7	7	ס	(15)	7	7
		8	8			8	8
	Total	15	15		Total	15	15
ע	(15)	7	7	ע	(16)	8	8
		8	8			7	7
	Total	15	15		Total	15	15
פ	(16)	8	8	פ	(17)	8	8
		8	8			7	7
	Total	16	16		Total	15	15
צ	(17)	8	8	צ	(18)	8	8
		9	9			9	9
	Total	17	17		Total	17	17
ר?	(18)	8	8	ק	(19)	9	9
		8	8			8	8
	Total	16	16		Total	17	17
ר	(19)	8	8	ר	(20)	6	6
		9	9			10	10
	Total	17	17		Total	16	16
ש	(20)	9	9	ש	(21)	6	6
		8	8			9	9
	Total	17	17		Total	15	15
ת	(21)	7	7	ת	(22)	7	7
		4	5			9	9
	Total	11	12		Total	16	16
פ	(22)	9	9	פ	(23)	8	8
		5	5			10	10
	Total	14	14		Total	18	18

Total Syllable Counts			
Psalm 25		Psalm 34	
Low	High	Low	High
367	381	373	375

symmetry in structure or quantity. Could this convergence in essentials and totals be the result of happenstance or random selection? We must describe and deduce the results and the overall picture by the actual evidence found in the text.

As the tables for these two psalms show, we do not have a precise syllable count for either of them, because of the difficulty in interpreting the evidence for the vocalization (hence the calculations of the 2d masculine singular pronominal suffixes attached to nouns, verbs, prepositions, and other parts of speech). As described and discussed elsewhere by us and others, the orthography in the MT favors the short form of the suffix (e.g., *āk*), and the vocalization occasionally (chiefly in the pausal position) conforms to and confirms such a reading. But in the great majority of cases, the Masoretes added a vowel after the final consonant (e.g., *-kā* or *-tā*), thus supplying an additional syllable. While this procedure is unusual and anomalous, it is not without precedent and, from other sources, including many of the Dead Sea Scrolls, it is clear that both the short and long forms were in use simultaneously in the language. Since in the MT the short spelling and the long pronunciation predominate, while we find a different mix in the Dead Sea Scrolls and other inscriptions, it is not easy to determine just how to vocalize the forms in Hebrew poetry or how to count the syllables. As a result we have counted these forms both ways and thus arrived at a low count and high count for the poems in which such 2d-person masculine singular forms occur. For the two psalms under consideration, the range for each is as follows:

	Psalm 25	*Psalm 34*
Low Count	367	373
High Count	381	375

The difference in the counts is entirely owing to the way in which the 2d-person masculine suffixes are treated. There are 14 such cases in Psalm 25 and only 2 in Psalm 34. It should be repeated that both long and short spellings are found in the MT, that is, *-k* and *-kh*, and both vocalizations, *-kā* and *-āk*. Where they correspond (i.e., *-kh* vocalized as *kâ* and *-k* as *-āk*) there is no problem, but where they diverge (*-k* vocalized as *-kā*), then it is difficult to decide what the practice of the poet or the original state of the text was. While we might in principle go with the spelling in preference to the vocalization, we cannot be sure of our ground, especially in view of the mixed evidence from the inscriptions, transcriptions, and scrolls. The fact that the Masoretes apparently structured their own rules and methods to accommodate the anomalous mixed texts (akin to *kethiv* /*qere* readings) suggests that the Masoretes believed the longer reading was more appropriate for literary and poetic texts than the shorter one.

For our purposes and the particular case of the two psalms under consideration here, we need not resolve this issue; however, we can recognize the existence of a spread in both cases between low count or high count—extensive in one case, minimal in the other—and draw the conclusion that both readings are possible, even likely, in both texts. Splitting the difference, we come out with a middle ground of 374 syllables for both poems, and this brings out the central point or thesis of this study—namely, that the paired poems will prove to be almost identical in overall length. This has been shown to be the case in regard to the first pair, Psalms 111 and 112 (170 syllables each), and now proves to be true of the second pair as well:

Psalm 25:	367–381, midpoint 374
Psalm 34:	373–375, midpoint 374

In both sets the overall length is exactly the same, although in neither cases does the total correspond to a fixed norm for such a poem. The norm for Psalms 111–112 should be 22 × 8 = 176, whereas the actual total for each psalm falls short by 6 syllables. In the cases of Psalms 25 and 34, we infer that the norm would be 23 × 16 = 368, whereas the actual total in each case is 374 (the average between low count and high count). If we go one step further and add the pairs, we get the following numbers:

Psalms 111	170	Psalm 112	170
Psalm 25	374	Psalm 34	374
Total	544	*Total*	544

In each case the norm would be 11 + 23 = 34 × 16 = 544. It is further to be noted that neither Psalm 25 nor Psalm 34 actually has 23 lines. Each has 22 lines but, in the case of Psalm 25, 2 lines are tricola (vv. 5 [ה] and 7 [ח]), while the rest are bicola, producing 46 cola or the equivalent of 23 lines or bicola. The case of Psalm 34 is more complicated, since there are only 22 lines, and all of them are bicola, making a total of 44 cola. Nevertheless, the total number of syllables in the poem is very close to that of Psalm 25. Only the method of getting to this result was different. Instead of adding whole cola, as is done in Psalm 25 (compare Proverbs 31 for the addition of a cola in v. 15, or see the added lines in Lamentations 1 and 2), extra words and syllables have been added to several lines of Psalm 34 to produce the augmented total. Consequently, the equation between the poems is maintained, although the surface appearances are different.

The next point is equally important, namely, that the norm or pattern for the poet in each case is the augmented alphabetic acrostic of 23 lines rather than the standard alphabetic acrostic of 22 lines. The second *peh* line at the end of the poem is considered a plus, even though in each case another line has been subtracted from the poem (the *waw* lines, a feature linking the poems, as noted above). While this reduces the total to 22 lines and seems to restore the appearance of the standard alphabetic acrostic of 22 lines (with the changes in order and identification of the lines themselves), the poet in each case has added the equivalent of a whole line to the poem. In this respect the treatment is the same as that accorded to Lamentations 1, 2, and 3, where the first two poems have one extra line, making a total of 67 against the standard or expected 66 lines. Chap. 3 has the standard 66 lines, but the total number of syllables has been increased to equal that of the first two chapters, confirming that the model for the poet has 67 lines and that chap. 3 has been filled out to match the totals of the first two chapters. It is the same here.

Psalms 9/10 and 37

We turn next to the third pair of psalms: Psalms 9/10 and Psalm 37. Here again the basic structure is the same in both psalms but with many variations and deviations in detail between them. Again, these two alphabetic acrostic poems form a unique pair, since no others found in the Hebrew Bible share the basic feature (the alphabetic bicolon or 4-colon structure). The only similar poem is Lamentations 4, which has 2-line stanzas, but the quantitative base is distinctly different because the average line length in Lamentations 4 is at least 2 syllables less than is the case with these psalms (13+ versus 16).

As in the previous cases, one member of the pair is more regular than the other, and we can use it (in this case Psalm 37) to establish the basic patterns and norms for the two psalms. What we would expect to begin with is an alphabetic sequence of 22 letters and 2-line units composing a 44-line or 88-colon poem. What we find is somewhat different, but the variations and deviations derive from the same single model.

In Psalm 37, there is a full complement of the letters of the alphabet in the regular order, with one noticeable exception. The couplet beginning with the letter *ʿayin* poses a problem, because between the *samek* unit and the *peh* unit (e.g., vv. 28–29) not a single word in the received text begins with the letter *ʿayin*, except for the last word in v. 29 (*ʿālеyhā*), which immediately precedes the first word of the *peh* unit: *pî*. Efforts to supply the missing *ʿayin* in an appropriate place, for example, in the middle of v. 28, require rather drastic emendation of the text and fail for that reason. As matters stand, the *samek* unit comprises 4 lines or 4 bicola and naturally divides in the following manner: v. 27 (bicolon); v. 28 (2 bicola); v. 29 (bicolon). It would be natural to take v. 28 with v. 27 as its complement or consequence, making a unit of 6 cola, which would be unusual but not unattested in the same poem. Note that the *ḥet* stanza has 3 bicola and 6 cola (vv. 14–15) and, while some scholars would like to erase half of v. 14 to reduce the stanza to the more-or-less standard 4 cola or 2 bicola, there is no necessity or even reason to do so. This leaves us v. 29 for the *ʿayin* unit or a single bicolon, otherwise unattested in this poem (although in the comparison with Psalms 9/10 we find the *yod* unit with 1 bicolon [9:18]). It is followed by *kap*, which has 6 cola or 3 bicola, a suitable correspondent to the situation in Psalm 37, namely a pair of units, one of which has 6 cola, while the other has only 2, making a combination with a total of 8 cola, equivalent to the normal count. The only difference is that the 6-colon unit precedes the bicolon in Psalm 37, whereas the reverse is the case in Psalms 9/10.

In both cases, the units form a coherent sequence, showing that the elements belong together and hence form a combination that conforms to the overall pattern but with a characteristic deviation. A further alteration occurs in Psalm 37, in the matter of the alphabetic pattern. Here we suggest that the letter (*ʿayin*) is not missing but precisely at the end of the whole unit, rather than its usual or expected place at the beginning of the second component. Thus the whole combination is bounded by *ṣûr* at the beginning of v. 27 and *ʿāleyhā* at the end of v. 29. Unusual? Certainly. Impossible? Hardly, and better than breaking up v. 28 or emending the text. Is there any other evidence for this kind of playful bending of the rules, or are we making a scribal error into a creative variation on the part of the poet? There is more evidence, and we shall return to this point.

In the meantime we wish to point out other variations from the standard scheme of 2 bicola or 4 cola per letter of the alphabet in Psalm 37.

In v. 7 the opening unit may be construed as a very short pair of cola or a single long one (i.e., 2 + 2 or 4, according to accents). In view of the preceding pair of cola, which have 3 accents each and 8 and 7 syllables respectively, it is more likely that we should read v. 7 as a tricolon rather than as a pair of bicola: 9 (4) + 8 (3) + 7 (3) = 24 syllables, 10 accents. It is noteworthy that we find almost the identical structure in 37:34 for the letter *qop*, where the first unit is either a short bicolon or a single colon (2 + 2 or 4 accents, 5 + 5 = 10 syllables), which is followed by a regular bicolon with 3 + 3 = 6 accents and 9 + 9 syllables.

One other tricolon occurs in the poem, the *kap* unit at v. 20. In spite of scholarly efforts to produce 4 cola, the natural division of the elements produces a tricolon:

7 syllables	3 accents
7 syllables	4 accents
7 syllables	3 accents

The situation is similar to what we found in the other two cases of tricola, but here, while the longer line could be divided into two pairs, there is only one verb and it is difficult to make sense out of the second part if it is separated from the first.

As noted earlier, the *ḥet* stanza has 6 cola or 2 more than the norm. This excess is balanced by the apparent reduction in the case of vv. 7 and 20, so the first half of the poem (vv. 1–20) balances out at 44 cola, the expected norm.

In the second half, we find a unit with 5 cola (vv. 25–26, the *nun* stanza). This expanded stanza is balanced by the tricolon in v. 34, which has been mentioned earlier. The only other variation occurs at the very end of the poem, where in v. 40 a single colon has been added at the end of v. 40, which then becomes a tricolon and makes the *taw* stanza a unit with 5 cola:

v. 39:	10 syllables	3 accents
	7 syllables	3 accents
v. 40:	11 syllables	3 accents
	12 syllables	3 accents
	4 syllables	2 accents

This poem shows many more variations in structure and pattern than earlier poems in our study, especially the unusual placement of a key alphabetic letter at the end rather than at the beginning of its stanza or unit. If this is not just a scribal accident, we might expect to find much more variation or irregularity in the companion piece, Psalms 9/10. Nevertheless, the two belong together and, as we can anticipate, they not only form a unique pair in the Hebrew Bible but have structural links that reinforce the idea that the end results are deliberate.

Therefore in Psalms 9/10, not only are the irregularities greater in number and extent, but some scholars doubt whether the text is really sound, and they suspect that this poem has suffered significant change both peripherally (i.e., at the level of the alphabet) and internally.

In spite of gaps and omissions, there can be no doubt that the poem here is a true alphabetic acrostic. At least 15 or 16 of the letters are represented and in the proper order, and for the most part each stanza has 4 cola in accordance with the underlying pattern. Nevertheless, the variations and deviations are so much more profound and radical in this poem than the earlier ones studied, even compared to its counterpart, that we must be very attentive to the shifts and consider constantly what may have been done on purpose and what may well be the result of scribal oversight or editorial misinterpretation.

The first major discrepancy or departure is the omission of the *dalet* unit. The *gimel* stanza (v. 6) is followed directly by the *he'* component (v. 7 *h'wyb*). A further variation is the reduction of the *gimel* unit to a single bicolon, while the *he'* unit extends over at least 4 cola and possibly (or probably) 6. The problem is that vv. 8, 9, 10, and 11 all begin with *waw*, which is the next letter after *he*ʾ, but this circumstance leaves us in a quandary as to exactly where the *waw* stanza begins. If we assume that the *waw* unit is normal and contains the usual 2 bicola, then the unit begins with *wyhy* in v. 10, which leaves vv. 7–9 for the *he*ʾ unit. Taking 6 with vv. 7–9, we have a structure very similar to the combination already identified in vv. 18–21 of this psalm, in which the *yod* unit has one bicolon and is followed by *kap* (vv. 19–21) with 6 cola. In all this, however, we should remember that the fourth letter, *dalet*, has simply disappeared.

In the second half of the poem, the first letter, *lamed*, does not seem to have a clear or certain successor until *qop* in v. 12, after which the sequence is regular, including 4 cola per stanza, through *reš*, *šin*, and *taw* until the end of the poem. The letters *peh* and *ʿayin* (in that order) seem to be present in vv. 7 and 8, and a case can be made, we think, for *mem*, *nun*, and later *ṣadeh*, but *samek* (like *dalet*) seems to be gone for good.

There are 21 cola between the presumed end of the *lamed* unit (10:2) and the beginning of the *qop* unit (10:12). This would allow for 5 letters, 4 with normal couplets (4 cola) and one with 5 cola, or some arrangement like that, and as a result we might be able to find the units for all of the intervening letters with the exception of one. So we have 5 letters accounted for and 5 more possible, omitting one out of an expected total of 11, as also in the case of the first half of the poem (Psalm 9), in which 10 letters are accounted for, while one (*dalet*) is missing. Since the fourth letter is missing in the first half, we suggest that the missing letter in the second part is *samek* (also the fourth letter).

We have already noted that the *lamed-mem* sequence takes up vv. 1–4: the first word in v. 1 begins with *lamed* (*lāmâ*), while the last word of v. 4 begins with *mem* (*mĕzimmōtāyw*). The unit is a double couplet with 4 bicola, or 8 cola in all, and therefore conforms to the standard pattern for a poem of this type. A similar combination of letters may be found in the *ʿayin-ṣadeh* pair in vv. 8c–11, beginning with the first word after the *ʾatnaḥ*, *ʿênāyw*, and closing with the last word of v. 11, *lāneṣaḥ*. We must suppose that the order of the alphabet adopted for this poem is different from the usual one, in reversing *peh* and *ʿayin*, but this reversal is also attested in Lamentations 2–4 (in contrast with Lamentations 1, where the normal order, *ʿayin peh*, is followed).

While *lnṣḥ* does not begin with *ṣadeh*, at least the letter itself is in the word, and it closes the unit, since the next unit begins with *qop* at the beginning of v. 12 (*qûmâ*).

Next we can identify the *peh* unit in vv. 7–8 (to the *ʾatnaḥ*) beginning with *pîhû*, the second word in v. 7. Whether the preceding word, *ʾālâ*, should be attached to the preceding unit or belongs with *pîhû* and the following words is not clear, although if we begin this unit with *pîhû*, then v. 7ab forms an excellent bicolon with strong structural parallelism.

That leaves us with vv. 5–6, which in our estimation should constitute the *nun* unit. The conclusion comes partly, perhaps largely, because the only other letter that could fit in here is *samek*, which does not occur at all in these verses. It is true that *samek* does show up in vv. 8–9 (e.g., *bmstrym* [v. 8] and *bmstr* and *bskh* [v. 9]), but this circumstance can hardly help us with vv. 5–6. If this is the *nun* unit of the poem, then the only candidate for this honor is the word *minnegdô*, which is under the major pause (*ʾatnaḥ*) in v. 5. Admittedly it is a slender thread on which to hang an alphabetic acrostic, but for this poet variation and deviation seem to be a ruling passion, if not a total way of life.

With these observations, our pursuit of this alphabetic acrostic psalm has come to a halt. Most of the letters are represented in their usual order, although *peh* and *ʿayin* are reversed; but this shift is attested elsewhere, revealing some uncertainty about the accepted sequence of those letters.

We confirm as well the omission of at least 2 letters of the alphabet as the poem has come down to us: the *dalet* unit seems clearly to be missing, and we think that this is true of *samek*, each occupying the fourth place in its half of the alphabet. Presumably the poet had a reason for this practice, but it would be difficult to identify the reason or purpose. We may leave that to others to investigate.

The major reason, in our opinion, for supposing that the poem is complete (although we cannot affirm with equal confidence that the poem is intact and that all the words are in their proper place or even that we have the right ones everywhere) is that in spite of all the omissions, or apparent displacements, the poem as a whole is very nearly the same length as the other poem of the same type and structure in the Psalter, Psalm 37. While the numbers are not quite as exact as for the other pairs of poems already examined, they nevertheless confirm that these two poems form an equivalent pair:

	Low Count	*High Count*
Psalm 37	326 + 341 + 48 = 715	329 + 349 + 49 = 727
Psalms 9/10	339 + 334 + 44 = 717	350 + 348 + 45 = 743
	665 + 675 + 92 = 1432	679 + 697 + 94 = 1470

The totals are almost identical at the low end, but there is a larger gap at the high end, owing to the higher number of pronominal suffixes in Psalms 9/10 than in Psalm 37. The averages or midpoints are as follows:

Psalm 37:	721
Psalms 9/10:	730

The grand totals would be as follows:

Low Count	1432
High Count	1470
Total	2902
Average or Median	1451

The average for each Psalm should reflect a colon count of 90 (for Psalm 37) or 91 (for Psalms 9/10), that is, 8 × 90 = 720 (Psalm 37) or 8 × 91 = 728 (Psalms 9/10). In practice we have isolated 89 cola in Psalm 37 (the single tricolon is to be found in 37:40, with the closing clause, *kî ḥāsû bô* [compare the closing of Ps 34:33, *kol-haḥōsîm bô*] which, however, is part of the second colon of that verse rather than constituting a separate element). Nevertheless, determining colon boundaries and hence the number of cola in a stanza or a poem is not an exact science, and there would be at least two other opportunities to divide a passage currently listed as a single colon into 2 cola: v. 9b would be a plausible candidate with the third colon beginning with the interruptive *hēmmâ*: 8 + 5 + 6 = 19 syllables in all. Another possibility is to read 34a as 2 cola and as a result v. 34 as a double bicolon, rather than the tricolon we have adopted. Not only are there two separate, coordinate clauses, but the syllable count is sufficient to sustain such a division: 5 + 5 = 10. For Psalm 37, the minimum colon count would be 89, and the maximum would be 91. A compromise at 90 seems appropriate.

Regarding Psalms 9/10, the situation is much more complicated, and the range between minimum and maximum counts of cola is proportionately similar to that of the syllables. The minimum count would be 84, while the maximum would be the same 91 that we noted for Psalm 37. The potential candidates for dividing or splitting would be the following: 9:11 is a reasonable candidate for division into 4 cola instead of the standard 2:

11a:	6 + 6 = 12
11b:	5 + 6 = 11

Ps 9:16 provides another opportunity for the same sort of division, especially in view of the occurrence of 2 verbs in both halves of the verse.

16a:	5 + 4 = 9
16b:	6 + 5 = 11

Then in chap. 10 we note the following cases: 10:2 could be divided as follows:

10:2a	5 + 4 = 9
10:2b	8 + 4 = 12

The same applies to 10:3.

10:3a 5 + 5 = 10
10:3b 5 + 4 = 9

The remaining possibility is to be found in 10:18 where, as might be expected in the last line of the poem, there is an extension. Here we find the extra colon (= clause) in the latter part of 18a, so we divide as follows: 7 + 4 + 8 = 19.

The maximum possible addition to the basic 84 cola would be 9, for a total of 93 cola, which is manifestly too high. In our judgment, we should accept the following: 9:11 and 16; either 10:2 or 3 (we lean toward v. 3 as a better candidate) and 10:18, for a total of 7 additional cola, bringing our total to 91 for Psalms 9/10.

We may now summarize the findings to date.

Psalm	*Cola per Letter*	*Letters*	*Lines*	*Cola*	*Syllables*
111	1	22	11	22	170
112	1	22	11	22	170
25	2	22	22	46	374
34	2	22	22	46	374
37	4	22	44	90	721
9/10	4	(20)	42	91	730
	14	130	152	317	2539

Psalms 119 and 145

We must now proceed to put the remaining pieces in place. The next poem in the Psalter is the Great Psalm, 119. Since we undertake a detailed study of this psalm in chaps. 2 and 3 below, there is no need to repeat the details and the arguments here. A summary of the totals may be offered, however.

	Low Count	*High Count*
Psalm 119	1417 + 1222 = 2639	1531 + 1371 = 2902

The structure of the psalm is fairly rigid: there are 22 stanzas, 1 for each letter of the alphabet in the standard sequence, and each stanza has 8 lines, each of which begins with the same specified letter (the first stanza has 8 lines, each beginning with *ʾalep*; the second stanza has the same pattern, with each line beginning with *bet*, and so on). While the number of lines is fixed at 176, the number of cola is less certain, and some tricola may be identified in order to reach an appropriate total.

This psalm comes next in the sequence, as indicated above: after pairs of psalms with half, single, and double lines, or 1, 2, and 4 cola respectively, we would expect two psalms with stanzas of 4 lines or 8 cola each, or a single psalm combining the 2 intermediate stanzas and thus representing the peak, climax, and conclusion of the series, which Psalm 119 certainly does. If, as we believe, Psalm 119 was designed to match up with the totals for all of the other alphabetic acrostic psalms, we note a minor but significant discrepancy in the totals for the six psalms just considered and Psalm 119. The total number of lines in the six psalms is 152, and the number of cola for each letter of the alphabet is 14, whereas the numbers in these categories of Psalm 119 are, respectively, 176 and 16. Therefore, while Psalm 119 is the next in order in the apparent arithmetic and especially geometric sequence, its totals will exceed those of the six preceding psalms. In order to balance out this deficiency or discrepancy, we observe that there is an eighth and final psalm in the Psalter that provides the missing numbers and makes up the difference between the six smaller psalms and the one Great Psalm. Psalm 145 is another alphabetic acrostic psalm, with 1 line and 2 cola per letter of the alphabet, basically similar to Psalms 25 and 34, but without the special features noted in those two poems.

In the interest of clarity and in order to fill out the picture for the smaller psalms, we will provide the essential information about Psalm 145. As already indicated, it conforms to the standard (and most frequent) of the alphabetic acrostic poems in the Bible—that is, a single line, double colon for each letter of the alphabet. Psalm 145 has its own peculiarities and idiosyncrasies, however, and these need to be noted. Psalm 145, like Psalms 25 and 34, omits one letter of the alphabet but a different one (*nun* instead of *waw*), and it does not add a letter-line at the end after the *taw* line. It may be that the omission in Psalm 145 was accidental or inadvertent, because a *nun*-line does occur in this psalm in the Psalm Scroll from Qumran Cave 11, and the latter is the oldest text of the psalm available to us (from the 1st century B.C.E., in all likelihood). We have no such restorations of the missing lines in the other psalms. Nevertheless, it is not an easy decision because the restoration, while an appropriate line in itself and supported by the LXX and Syriac translations, may nevertheless be a secondary addition to what was naturally regarded as a defective text. It is not easy to decide such matters, so we will give data for both versions of the psalm.

	Low Count	*High Count*
Psalm 145 (MT)	174 + 195 = 378	186 + 208 + 5 = 399
Psalm 145 (with *nun*)	183 + 207 + 5 = 395	195 + 216 + 5 = 416

We are now ready to assemble the table for the seven minor alphabetic acrostic psalms, providing the necessary information about lines, cola, and syllables (table 4).[7]

Table 4. Seven Minor Alphabetic Acrostic Psalms

Psalm	*Cola per letter*	*Letters*	*Lines*	*Cola*	*Syllables*	*Words*	*–Heading*	=	*Body of Poem*
9/10	4 (2)	20	42	91	730	327	– 5	=	322
25	2 (1)	22	22	46	374	159	– 1	=	158
34	2 (1)	22	22	46	374	165	– 8	=	157
37	4 (2)	22	44	90	721	298	– 1	=	297
111	1 (1/2)	22	11	22	170	74	– 2	=	72
112	1 (1/2)	22	11	22	170	79	– 2	=	77
145	2 (1)	21 (or 22)	21 (or 22)	47/8	389/406	152/9	– 2	=	150/7
Total	16 (8)	22	173 (or 174)	364/6	2928/45	1254/61	– 21	=	1233/40

We may compare the collection of seven psalms with the Great Psalm, 119. It will be noted that in each category there is a correlation between Psalm 119 and the others taken as a group, whether in the total number of lines or cola, or lines and cola per alphabetic letter, or finally, in syllables.

Regarding Psalm 119, we give the numbers derived from the earlier articles and add the numbers that are relevant to this study. The number of lines and cola per letter is fixed by the structure of the psalm: 8 lines and 16 cola. The total number of lines is determined by the stanza structure and the alphabetic repetition: 22 stanzas with 8 lines each are 176 lines. When it comes

7. As with several other of these psalm, there is some uncertainty about the number of cola. Probably the phrase at the end of the last verse (21), *lĕʿôlām wāʿed,* should be regarded as a 3d colon, echoing the same phrase that occurs at the beginning of the psalm (at the end of v. 1). The phrase is repeated at the end of v. 2, and all 3 can be construed in the same manner. Other possible cola may be found in v. 3a

$$4 + 6 = 10$$

and in v. 15b

$$3 + 2 + 2 = 7$$
$$1 + 2 + 3 = 6$$

Thus we may add as many as 2 cola to the total for this psalm:

47 for Psalm 145 in the MT, or
49 if we add the *nun* line.

to counting cola, while most lines have the expected 2 cola, some seem to be tricola, as noted:

1.	v. 23	6+4+9 = 19
2.	v. 39	5+5+7 = 17
3.	v. 43	6+7+9 = 22
4.	v. 48	10+5+8 = 23
5.	v. 62	6+5+7 = 18
6.	v. 63	4+8+9 = 21
7.	v. 69	8+5+6 = 19
8.	v. 75	5+6+8 = 19
9.	v. 78	5+6+9 = 20
10.	v. 145	6+5+6 = 17
11.	v. 169	5+6+9 = 20
12.	v. 176	7+5+9 = 21

Some of our tricola-line conjectures are more persuasive than others, but a reasonable case can be made for at least half (6) of them, which is the compromise we have adopted elsewhere. Added to the basic 352, that gives us 358 cola, while if we added all of them (12), the total of 364 would be very close to the total for all of the other psalms together. When it comes to syllable counts, the minimum and maximum counts for the Great Psalm range from 2639 to 2902; or, for the various reasons we adopted, 2815 may be the best approximation. Let us look at the numbers once more and then draw come conclusions.

	Lines	*Cola*	*Letters*	*Lines*	*Cola*	*Syllables*	*Words*
Group of 7	8	16	22	173/4	364/6	2928/45	1233/40
Psalm 119	8	16	22	176	352-364	2639/2902	1065

At a minimum, we can say that this group of 8 psalms is more than a haphazard or accidental collection based only on the common use of the alphabet as an organizing principle. Certainly this is their most prominent feature, but it is far from being the only one. The grouping in pairs is equally striking, and the gradation from half-line units to the 8-line unit through intermediate arithmetic and geometric stanzas betokens a more complex assemblage and interconnection among the members of the group.

The basic division with four psalms in the first book (2 pairs in an envelope construction 9/10[2], 25[1], 34[1], 37[2]) and four more in the last book (111 and 112 forming the third pair, with the last two [119 and 145] making up an odd couple to complete the overall symmetry) reflects the editor's sense of design. Then we may take the seven smaller psalms as a group, which matches up quite nicely with the Great Psalm itself, sharing several basic features: number of lines, cola per letter, the overall number of lines and cola, and finally an approximate match in both words and syllables. Within the larger symmetrical composite, we find numerous deviations and variations from the presumed norm. It is not always easy or even possible to distinguish deliberate alterations from errors in copying: for example, we believe the omission of the *waw* lines from Psalms 25 and 34 to be quite deliberate, correlating with the equally deliberate addition of *peh* lines at the end of each of these psalms. At the same time, the presence of the word *rĕʾēh* in the beginning of v. 18 in Psalm 25, where we expect a word beginning with the letter *qop*, seems to be a copyist's error (vertical dittography), since the same word begins the next verse (v. 19) correctly. Other instances, such as the omission of the *nun* line in Psalm 145, are less certain, and no firm decision is reached about these.

In most cases, the numbers offer convincing support to the idea that the matching psalms really match, in spite of numerous differences in detail: note the almost identical lengths (in syllable counts) for each of the pairs 111/112 and 25/34. In the case of Psalms 37 and 9/10, the differences in detail are much greater, and Psalms 9/10 especially seem to have suffered internal damage, resulting in the loss of more than one letter (maybe several). In spite of this, the psalm is almost the same length as the apparently undamaged parallel psalm, 37.

The addition of Psalm 145 to the group was apparently intended to fill out the gap in numbers between the three pairs and the Great Psalm (119). The sequence in lineation (i.e., cola per letter of the alphabet)—1 (Pss 111 and 112); 2 (Pss 25 and 34); 4 (Pss 9/10 and 37); 16 (Ps 119)—produced a gap in the symmetry, since the first three pairs add up to 14 cola per letter, whereas Psalm 119 necessarily has 16, so the difference is made up in the added psalm, which has 1 line or 2 cola per letter. Thus the gap is filled, the symmetry restored, and the whole group presented as a master work of unity and integrity, faithfully reflecting the two great activities of God: the creation in eight stages or works, and the Torah or the Word, recorded in the Bible and expressed in the alphabetic psalms. The Great Psalm, revolving around the number *eight*, is a celebration of the Torah (and its seven sister and brother key-words), while the seven lesser psalms celebrate the whole gamut of divine activity and presence in his universe.

Chapter 2
The Structure of Psalm 119: Part I

David Noel Freedman

[[725]] Psalm 119 in the Hebrew Bible is a mechanical and technical marvel. Traditionally called "The Great Psalm," it has always been recognized as not only the longest single poem in the Psalter, but also the most consistently sustained piece of poetic rhetoric in the Bible, a constant and repeated meditation on the theme of "the teaching of Yahweh" (*tôrat yahweh*, v. 1), a testimony that recurs in almost every line of the poem. In the present paper, I will discuss the structure of the psalm in general, and in particular its alphabetic acrostic pattern, including the selection and distribution of its key words.

The thesis that I will advocate and support with data and arguments is that the poem has an essentially simple symmetrical structure based on the alphabet, but also that the poet has built into and upon this easily identified and recognized structure a series of refinements and elaborations, of deliberate variations and deviations from established norms, the latter having been largely ignored or misconstrued by scholars in the past. For example, it is universally accepted that there are 8 key words in the poem (*tôrâ*, the first among equals, and 7 other terms with similar meaning) and that most of the lines of the poem contain one of these words. It has been observed that 4 lines, and 4 only, conspicuously do not contain any of these words, and typically (cf. BHS critical notes) scholars propose to emend each of those 4 lines by altering other words to conform [[726]] to the governing pattern of the poem.[1]

Reprinted, with permission, from *Pomegranates and Golden Bells: Studies in Biblical, Jewish, and Near Eastern Ritual, Law, and Literature in Honor of Jacob Milgrom* (ed. David P. Wright, David Noel Freedman, and Avi Hurvitz; Winona Lake, Ind.: Eisenbrauns, 1995) 725–56. Original pagination is marked by page number in [[ ]].

1. "Emendation based on pattern is admittedly risky, but rarely in biblical Hebrew does one encounter a pattern as consistent as this. No convincing reasons have been given as to why the psalmist should depart in vv. 3, 37, 90 and 122 from a pattern employed so

Such an approach and such treatment are understandable but in this instance at least shortsighted. The point is that while 167 lines of the 176 in the poem have one of the key words each and 4 of the lines have none, the remaining 5 lines have 2 of the key words and thus make up for the deficiency. So the total expected number of 176 is made up in this variation or deviation from the established pattern. The poet, therefore, is not guilty of an oversight that modern scholars have the right or obligation to rectify, and scribes are not to blame for miscopying the text, but the whole scheme is quite deliberate, with the deficiency of 4 words being made up for by adding 4 words in other lines. By applying this principle of compensation, the poet has added an intricacy or a complexity to an otherwise very simple pattern but in so doing has left behind many of his interpreters.

There is still another twist to be considered, and this is the addition of one more key word beyond the expected total of 176 to match up with the number of lines. Does the presence of the 177th example of a key word reflect a breakdown in this elaborate scheme, and may we finally say that the single extra word is the result of a scribal error (i.e., dittography, a common error)? Or is this yet a final punctuation mark in a very sophisticated juggling or balancing act on the part of the poet, that is, a deliberate distortion at the end to make the listener or reader take notice? Is the resultant distributional pattern a distant echo of the familiar device, known from the Ugaritic poems and many biblical ones as well, of a numerical sequence: X // X + 1 (e.g., Amos 1–2, "For three transgressions, yea for four . . . ")? Thus, as expected, we have exactly 88 key words in the first half of the poem (vv. 1–88) and 88 + 1 = 89 occurrences in the second half of the poem (vv. 89–176). The issues will be discussed in greater detail later on, but the immediate lesson is that often the poet is far beyond any kind of simplistic notions about parallelism and symmetry: they are present and pervasive, but the deviations and variations are also ubiquitous. What fascinates is the way in which the poet manages to establish and maintain the underlying and overarching patterns and at the same time seems to lose his grip and wander off the [[727]] defined limits; but in fact everything balances out and we can only applaud the artist and his finished work. It is like a high-wire act in a circus, where the acrobat after establishing himself on the wire, initiates a series of maneuvers that become more

---

consistently elsewhere, and only minor emendation of the consonantal text is required to bring these verses into line with this pattern" (W. Soll, *Psalm 119: Matrix, Form and Setting* [CBQMS 23; Washington: Catholic Biblical Association, 1991] 52).

A useful synopsis of scholarly reconstructions of Psalm 119, beginning with Muller, is provided by J. D. Levenson, "The Sources of Torah: Psalm 119 and the Modes of Revelation in Second Temple Judaism," *Ancient Israelite Religion* (ed. P. D. Miller, P. D. Hanson, and S. D. McBride; Philadelphia: Fortress, 1987) 559–74.

complicated and dangerous as he proceeds, drawing gasps of fear and astonishment from the audience, and seems on the brink of falling but manages to hang on, and brings the whole house down with a final impossible feat. Or we may think of a master juggler, who having started with the usual hoops and balls, manages to keep adding more and more objects to his repertoire and at the same time climbs on a chair that is balanced on one leg, juggles with different parts of his body: arms, legs, head; seems on the point of losing everything, and then miraculously collects everything piece by piece, including the chair, makes his bow and departs to sustained applause, while people wonder just how he did it all. The same is true of this poet and his poem. Just when we think we have found a mistake, an omission, an insertion, an accidental alteration, or even an editorial change, it turns out to be a deliberate deviation from the norm, and what looks like a defect turns out to be part of a more sophisticated rearrangement of the parts. This does not necessarily mean that there are no errors or that scribes have miraculously preserved the text intact. There are too many variant readings among the extant Hebrew manuscripts (especially the *Psalms Scroll* from Cave 11)[2] and between the Hebrew tradition and the Septuagint to make any extravagant claims about the integrity or sanctity of the preserved text. One of the most difficult tasks of all is to distinguish between an error in transmission and deliberate deviation. On the whole, modern scholars have been too eager to emend, but we should not revert to the older style that rejected the possibility of error and the necessity for emendation in the face of convincing, even overwhelming evidence of a defect in the transmitted text. A cautious, conservative approach is obligatory, in my judgment, but in the end we may have to leave certain issues open and without a firm conclusion. These and other details will be treated at greater length in the body of the paper, but generally speaking, the fully developed and highly sophisticated end product has not been sufficiently appreciated as an example and symbol of the technical precision and expertise of at least one major Hebrew poet, especially in the latter days of the biblical period. And in passing we may observe that to make the claim, as many scholars have done and still do, that a poet, who clearly counted practically everything that could be counted in such a poem as this (including stanzas, lines, key [[728]] words, pronominal suffixes, etc.), would not or did not count syllables, as so many poets in so many other languages have done routinely, seems somewhat questionable, not to say faintly ridiculous.

As has always been recognized, Psalm 119 represents an apotheosis or ultimate expression of the alphabetic acrostic pattern in Hebrew biblical poetry. A number of other examples occur in the Psalter and elsewhere in the Bible.

2. J. A. Sanders, *The Dead Sea Psalms Scroll* (Ithaca, N.Y.: Cornell University Press, 1967).

Some embody the alphabetic pattern in single cola (see Psalms 111, 112) and others in standard bicola (e.g., Psalms 25, 34, 145), while still others are more elaborate (see Psalms 9–10, 37; Lamentations 1–4); in addition there are poems that follow the same structure as the alphabetic acrostic psalms but do not retain the alphabetic feature (see Lamentations 5 for a recognized example, as well as Psalm 33).[3] Certainly Psalm 119 is the most elaborate and ingeniously devised of the entire group, combining in effect eight parallel alphabetic acrostic poems in a single majestic composition, a concentrated meditation on the single central theme: *tôrat yhwh* (v. 1) // *miṣwōt ʾĕlōhāy* (v. 115).

Briefly stated, the poem consists of 22 stanzas, one for each letter of the Hebrew alphabet in the traditional order. Typically, in all of the alphabetic acrostic poems in the Bible there is only one entry or unit for the letters *śin/šin* (the same letter with different pointing), so the system was clearly visual rather than aural, since *ś/š* forms are mixed in this poem: thus although we would expect the letter *šin* to predominate, the actual distribution in Psalm 119 is *śin* beginning lines 161–62 and 166, while *šin* begins lines 163–65, 167–68. Each stanza has 8 lines (= verses in this poem), and the first word of each line begins with the same appropriate letter of the alphabet. Thus the 8 lines of the first stanza all begin with *ʾalep*, while each of the 8 lines of the second stanza begins with *bet*, and so on to the last stanza, whose 8 lines all begin with *taw*. There are no exceptions as far as the letters at the beginning of the lines are concerned, so that we may be reasonably sure that we have the complete poem as devised by the author, with its original intentional structure intact. This datum does not automatically guarantee that the poem has been preserved in perfect pristine condition, but it may serve as a caution against excessive freewheeling emendation of the text as scholars seek to maintain or improve its balance or symmetry. The variant readings in the *Psalms Scroll* from Cave 11 at Qumran, compared to the MT and the divergences in the LXX and other versions, show that there have been at least minor changes and doubtless some errors in the course of transmission, but they do not affect the overall structure or the division of the poem into its [[729]] constituent parts, in particular the stanzas and lines (= verses, or bicola). We have the correct number of both for this lengthy composition.

One further comment about the basic structure of the poem may be in order. As already noted, the number of stanzas in the poem has been determined by the number of letters in the Hebrew alphabet, 22. This number, in turn, is divisible by 2, but then we reach the prime number 11, so no further integer-divisions are possible. Symmetry in construction, therefore, is limited to the simplest kind, one-to-one correspondence, or what I call bilateral parallelism.

3. D. N. Freedman, "Acrostics and Metrics in Hebrew Poetry," *Pottery, Poetry, and Prophecy* (Winona Lake, Ind.: Eisenbrauns, 1980) 51–76.

The two equal or balancing parts of the poem consist of 11 stanzas or 88 lines each. Any further division along these lines would necessarily divide a stanza in half and therefore would not be part of the original structure of the poem. Contrariwise, the number 8, equal to the number of lines in each stanza, is clearly and deliberately chosen by the poet, and reflecting the latter's interest in symmetry, is more easily divided into equal parts, whether by 2 or by 4, thus producing a multiplicity of possible parallel and equivalent units and subdivisions. As we shall see, the combination of 22 stanzas and 8 lines may be worked to provide any number of symmetrical constructions throughout the poem as a whole. While the number 8 may not carry as much content, portent, and symbolism as the number 7, it has uses and meanings of its own in the Bible and ancient Near Eastern literature. As the companion of the number 7 in Ugaritic and biblical poetry (i.e., 7 // 7 + 1), it also connotes completeness and totality and perfection and at the same time carries with it the connotations of the important number 4 (i.e., the 4 directions of the compass) only more so. Thus if, as we suppose, the poet was very much interested in describing and depicting totality and completeness (which begins with the alphabet, covering all the letters from *ʾalep* to *taw*, or *alpha* to *omega*, as would be said or written in Greek, or as we would say in English, from A to Z) as well as bilateral symmetry (the most characteristic expression of which would be the ubiquitous parallelism in Hebrew poetry) then he has chosen the numbers well. The poem divides easily into two equal and parallel parts, and then the number 8 may be used and divided in a variety of ways to reflect and reveal the intricate and complex pairing that occurs everywhere in the poem. We will use the principle of bilateral symmetry as a working hypothesis in exploring the structure of the poem and the distribution of its parts, based on the occurrence of this phenomenon throughout the literature of the Hebrew Bible, and especially in the form of parallelism in Hebrew poetry.

Before proceeding to a more detailed analysis of the poem, I will pause or digress briefly to establish or confirm what is already universally agreed upon, namely that this psalm is a piece of classic Hebrew poetry, ⟦730⟧ composed in conformance with whatever basic characteristics and principles we can isolate and identify in this rather difficult subject. I am not talking about the literary quality of the work (it is generally agreed to be rather pedestrian and mechanical in its content) but only about its technical aspects. It may well be late in date; along with most scholars, I regard it as postexilic and would place it in the fifth century, around the time of Ezra, not least because of its central preoccupation with the Torah of Yahweh, a dominant theme of the reformation engineered by the notable scribe.[4] Along with the very frequent use of

4. For two different reconstructions of the psalm's exilic or postexilic setting, see Soll, *Psalm 119*, 142–54, and Levenson, "Sources of Torah," 570–74.

parallelism, to which we have already alluded, we may point objectively to the very low "prose particle" count of this "late" poem. According to my calculations, which were made independently of Andersen and Forbes[5] but which are in full agreement with their work, there are 1065 words in this poem and a total of 17 prose particles (i.e., the relative pronoun *ʾăšer*, the *nota accusativi ʾet*, and the definite article *ha-*) giving us a percentage of 1.6%, which is extremely low by any standard. Thus there would not be a single prose passage of comparable length in the whole Bible that would come anywhere near this level. The ratio is at the low end even for poetry and compares well with the alphabetic acrostic poems in Lamentations, which are also exilic or postexilic in date (Lamentations 1–3 is in the range from 2.6% to 2.9%, while Lamentations 5 is at 1.4%). In other words, in postexilic times there are numerous examples of good classic Hebrew poetry, along with instances in which there are tendencies toward the mixture or the infiltration of a higher percentage of prose particles, as in the Song of Songs. Thus any piece of literature with a prose particle count of 2% or less is bound to be a poem, and the convergence of data and conclusions about Psalm 119 only serves to confirm both kinds of approaches to this material. Thus these numbers provide confirmation, if any were needed, that the universal opinion about this psalm is correct, and correspondingly the value and reliability of a simple objective and mechanical test of the material are supported by the uniformity of agreement about the nature of the work. The high correlation between alphabetic acrostic compositions, wherever they are found, and very low prose particle counts (i.e., under 5%) is consistently maintained for this poem and everywhere in the Bible.

⟦731⟧ As already affirmed by Will Soll and others before him, there are 8 and only 8 key nouns in the psalm, corresponding to the 8 lines in each stanza of the poem.[6] These words turn up regularly and repeatedly throughout the poem, so it has been a reasonable presumption on the part of readers, including scholars, that the correlation and combination are deliberate and that it was the intention of the poet to have one of these words in each line and to have all 8 represented in each stanza. In the end, then, each of these words would show up once in each stanza, or 22 times in all, and there would be a different word in each of the 176 lines of the poem. No doubt, this sort of ideal pattern was in the mind of the poet and was part of the basic struc-

5. F. I. Andersen and A. D. Forbes, " 'Prose-Particle' Counts of the Hebrew Bible," in *The Word of the Lord Shall Go Forth: Essays in Honor of David Noel Freedman in Celebration of His Sixtieth Birthday* (ed. C. Meyers and M. O'Connor; Winona Lake, Ind.: Eisenbrauns, 1983) 165–83.

6. Soll, *Psalm 119*, 35–48. See Levenson ("Sources of Torah," 562) for a defense of the theory that there are ten key words.

ture, along with the 22 stanzas and the 8 lines per stanza. This would mean 176 of the 8 words, distributed evenly among the stanzas at the rate of one per line. Overall, there is sufficient correspondence with the ideal pattern to show that the poet was consciously following a model or schema, but the deviations and variations are so extensive as to preclude the notion that these latter departures from the ideal norm are the result of transmissional errors or scribal oversights. The fact is that no two stanzas are exactly the same when it comes to the number and distribution of the key words, not one of the key words occurs in every one of the stanzas, and there are other exceptions and anomalies that vary widely from any simple application of the underlying principle of having 8 key words corresponding to the 8 lines of each stanza and the notion of equal and regular distribution through the poem. On the one hand there are actually 177 key words in the poem, which is so close to 176, the normative number, that we may be sure that the poet was fully aware of this correlation and intended it to be worked out, but we really cannot be sure whether the deviation by one is the result of an accidental copying error by some scribe (dittography, which is common enough in scribal transmission) or whether it is a deliberate action on the part of the poet to show among other things that he is not a slave to the structure of the poem but an independent creative artist.[7] On the other hand, the distribution of these 177 (or 176) key words, while corresponding generally to the scheme (that is, 167 lines actually contain one and only one key word, while 4 lines have none of them, and 5 lines have 2 of them), deviates from rigid uniformity so greatly and so often, that we must conclude that deviation and irregularity are just as important to the overall pattern of the poem (and the poet) as the symmetrical and simple basic structure of the poem. It is precisely [[732]] the combination of a simple underlying structure and a repetitive pattern with a very extensive series of departures from and distortions of that pattern that constitutes the operating method of the poet. The temptation to make the details conform to the pattern must be resisted if the true work of the poet and his peculiar and particular genius are to be acknowledged and properly appreciated. Thus it should come as no surprise that out of the 22 stanzas, only 4 follow the "correct" model in containing all 8 of the key words, and one each to a line. All of the other stanzas deviate in one respect or another, so for this principle at least, deviation and aberration are the norm rather than conformity to the basic, simple pattern of distribution. Similarly, we would expect each of the 8 words to occur 22 times, for an average of once per stanza, and overall this is true; but closer inspection shows that only 2 or 3 of the words actually occur 22 times, while the others diverge

7. Levenson (ibid.) cites B. Bonkamp's conclusion that there are 177 key words, anticipating our independent research by forty years.

from this number, and none of them is distributed evenly throughout the poem. Just as not one of the words (even those that occur 22 or more times) occurs in every stanza, so many of them turn up more than once in selected stanzas. While at first sight these seem to be clumsy mistakes, it is clear that they are so numerous and so deeply embedded in the structure of the poem, that the poem would have to be recomposed from scratch in order to make the actuality fit the system. We must recognize another and partially conflicting principle at work here, namely the deliberate distortion of a simple structure, the intentional deviation from the established norms, in order to produce a variety of effects, but mainly strain and pressures, to elicit different responses from the reader and student of the poem.

We may conclude as follows: About the basic structure or pattern there can be little question. It is simple and it is obvious, including the 8 key words corresponding to the 8 lines in each stanza. The poet, nevertheless, has freely modified the details of the plan to meet other objectives, among which we may postulate the desire to avoid monotony and endless regular repetition. At the same time, he is very much aware of the model adopted for the poem and ultimately brings the freewheeling departures into conformity with the underlying and overarching pattern, a major tour de force. The totals will come out right, and the basic bilateral symmetry will be visible: thus there are 88 key words in the first half of the poem and 88 + 1 = 89 in the second half. There is enough regularity and repetition (the numbers come out right in the end) to show that the patterns are there; at the same time there is enough deviation and distortion to show that the poet is manipulating his material against the underlying schema, to produce sophisticated effects that challenge the intelligence and subtlety of the reader. I shall try to show that there [[733]] is even a level at which the deviations contribute to a higher synthesis and uniformity; in other words, there is symmetry in variation. Often, when we think we have traced the subtleties of the poet to an end point, it turns out to be only a point of departure for yet one more twist, a departure from the norm at one level and yet part of a higher whole, a work of art as well as of artifice. What this sort of development shows is that the poet has deviated deliberately, even violently, but not randomly, thereby achieving a higher order of sophistication and intricacy than we have generally (or ever) attributed to the biblical poets.

The key words are all nouns (= substantives) and generally interchangeable, that is to say, synonyms. Listed alphabetically, they are as follows:

1. *ʾimrâ* ‘saying’
2. *dābār* ‘word’
3. *ḥōq* ‘statute’
4. *miṣwâ* ‘commandment’

5. *mišpāṭ* 'judgment'
6. *ʿēdôt* 'stipulations'
7. *piqqûd* 'regulation'
8. *tôrâ* 'law'

No effort is made here to define any of the terms accurately or adequately but only to distinguish them from each other by a roughly equivalent English expression. All of them revolve around a center, which is summed up in a phrase found in the very first verse of the poem: *tôrat yhwh* 'Yahweh's instruction'. We may translate the first verse as follows:

> Happy are those who are perfect in (the) way,
> those who walk in the Torah of Yahweh.

The centrality and preeminence of the word *tôrâ* are confirmed by the fact that it occurs more frequently than any other content word in the whole poem, 25 times. A close second is a companion word (*yhwh*), as seen in the first verse, where the combination *twrt yhwh* occurs (uniquely as it happens); see table 1 (p. 34). The word *yhwh* is clearly not one of the 8 key words, but certainly it is centrally important and occurs 24 times. Strangely enough, even though the main theme of the poem is precisely the *twrt yhwh*, the two words do not occur again together in a construct chain in the poem and only rarely in the same line of the poem. The theme is repeated endlessly however, not only by the use of the other 7 synonymous terms, but by the presence of the ubiquitous second masculine-singular pronominal suffix, which always represents Yahweh. This suffix is attached to the 8 key words repeatedly (including [[735]] *twrh*) and to many other words for a total of 225 occurrences in the poem, but the precise combination we have in v. 1 does not occur again. There is nevertheless a single phrase, the only other construct chain involving one of the key words and a divine appellative, which matches and balances the initial expression, *twrt yhwh*: it is *miṣwōt ʾĕlōhāy* 'the commandments of my God', which occurs in v. 115. It is to be noted that while we might have expected a phrase parallel to the central theme of the poem to be found either closer to the original (in v. 1 or close by) or at a place corresponding to it in the larger structure, that is, in the last line of the poem or the first line of the second part (corresponding to the principle of bilateral symmetry), it does occur in the second part, as expected, but hidden away in the recesses (v. 115).

This will be a recurring experience in our investigation of the poem. The point, nevertheless, is that there is a corresponding or matching expression, only one, and it comes up in the second half of the poem. It is also to be noted that *ʾĕlōhāy* is the only other divine title or name to be used in the whole poem, so that if we add the single instance of *ʾĕlōhîm* to the 24 instances of

YHWH AND TWRH Table 1

STANZA

Stanza	(ʾlhy) yhwh	twrt(k)	
1	(1) yhwh *1*	(1) twrt *1*	2
2	(4) yhwh *12*		1
3		(2) mtwrtk *18*	1
4	(7) yhwh *31*	(5) wtwrtk *29*	2
5	(1) yhwh *33*	(2) twrtk *34*	2
6	(1) yhwh *41*	(4) twrtk *44*	2
7	(4) yhwh *52* (7) yhwh *55*	(3) mtwrtk *51* (5) twrtk *53* (7) twrtk *55*	5
8	(1) yhwh *57* (8) yhwh *64*	(5) twrtk *61*	3
9	(1) yhwh *65*	(6) twrtk *70* (8) twrtk pyh *72*	3
10	(3) yhwh *75*	(5) twrtk *77*	2
11		(5) ktwrtk *85*	1
	[11] 11 yhwh	[13] 12 k 1 construct	24
12	(1) yhwh *89*	(4) twrtk *92*	2
13		(1) twrtk *97*	1
14	(3) yhwh *107* (4) yhwh *108*	(5) twrtk *109*	3
15	(3) ʾlhy *115*	(1) wtwrtk *113*	2
16	(6) lyhwh *126*	(6) twrtk *126*	2
17		(8) twrtk *136*	1
18	(1) yhwh *137*	(6) wtwrtk *142*	2
19	(1) yhwh *145* (5) yhwh *149* (7) yhwh *151*	(6) mtwrtk *150*	4
20	(4) yhwh *156* (7) yhwh *159*	(1) twrtk *153*	3
21	(6) yhwh *166*	(3) twrtk *163* (5) twrtk *165*	3
22	(1) yhwh *169* (6) yhwh *174*	(6) wtwrtk *174*	3
	[14] 13 yhwh 1 ʾlhy	[12] 12 k	26
	[25] 24 yhwh 1 ʾlhy	[25] 24 k 1 construct	[50]

SUMMARY
FIRST HALF + SECOND HALF = TOTAL

FREQUENCY IN STANZAS	twrh	yhwh (ʾlhy)
0	1 + 0 = 1	2 + 2 = 4
1	8 + 10 = 18	7 + 5 = 12
2	1 + 1 = 2	2 + 3 = 5
3	1 + 0 = 1	0 + 1 = 1

( ) = STANZA LINE NUMBER

[ ] = TOTAL

yhwh, we have the same total as the occurrences of *twrh*, as already noted, another example of match-ups or symmetry. As table 1 shows, the distribution of the words *twrh* and *yhwh* / *ʾlhy* seems to be relatively even throughout the poem, and in general they do not occur in the same line or verse. There are four instances in which they do, although except for v. 1 they never form a single combination. These instances are in lines 1, 55, 126, and 174, or in the 1st, 7th, 16th, and 22d stanzas, that is, 2 in the first half of the poem and 2 in the second. Furthermore the distribution is exactly symmetrical, understood as filling out an envelope construction. Thus, as we should expect, the 2 words occur in the last stanza of the poem, just as they do in the first stanza (it would be gauche, however, to put them in the last line of the last stanza, third from the end being quite sufficient for the poet to make his point).[8] The second occurrence is in the 7th stanza, or 6 from the first, while the third occurrence is in the 16th stanza, which in turn is 6 from the last stanza where the fourth occurrence of these 2 words is found. Correspondingly, the pair in the 7th stanza is 4 from the last stanza in the first part of the poem, and the pair in the 16th stanza is 4 from the beginning of the second part of the poem.

We may now proceed to a discussion of the remaining key words and then of all 8 of them together. As already noted, the 8 together constitute a separate group. They occur more frequently than any other content [[736]] words in the poem and are generally synonymous with or closely connected to the word *tôrâ*. We will list them again now, with their numerical frequencies, divided between the two halves of the poem:

Key Word	*Part A* (Stanzas 1–11)	*Part B* (Stanzas 12–22)	*Total*
1. *ʾimrâ*	8	11	19
2. *dābār*	11	11	22
3. *ḥōq*	14	8	22
4. *miṣwâ*	12	10	22
5. *mišpāṭ*	10	13	23
6. *ʿēdôt*	10	13	23
7. *piqqûd*	10	11	21
8. *tôrâ*	13	12	25
Total	88	89	177

8. D. N. Freedman, "The Twenty-Third Psalm," *Pottery, Poetry, and Prophecy* (Winona Lake, Ind.: Eisenbrauns, 1980) 275–302.

It should be noted immediately that four of the nouns are feminine and four are masculine, a clear instance of bilateral symmetry and also supporting the idea of totality and completeness, a theme deeply embedded in this poem through the use of the alphabet and the number 8. Less clear is the distinction between singular and plural. The distinction is quite clear with respect to the feminine nouns: two are always singular, namely *ʾimrâ* and *tôrâ*, while the other two are always plural: *miṣwôt* and *ʿēdôt* (there are in fact exceptions: thus we have *ʿēdût*, singular, in v. 88, and probably *miṣwōt* in v. 115 was originally intended to be singular, *miṣwat*, as the spelling in the *Psalms Scroll* from Cave 11 indicates; the spelling is *mṣwt*, which is normal for the singular in this scroll, instead of the usual spelling of the plural which would be *mṣwwt*).[9] The MT has the spelling *mṣwt* throughout, and the only way to tell the difference between singular and plural is by the vocalization: *miṣwat* for the singular and *miṣwōt* for the plural. Since in v. 115 *mṣwt ʾlhy* matches *twrt yhwh* in v. 1, it may well be that *mṣwt* was understood to be in the singular to correspond to the singular *tôrâ*. Furthermore in v. 16 we have the word *ḥuqqōtêkā* instead of the expected *ḥuqqêkā*, showing that inevitably and frequently there are exceptions to any and all patterns of repetition in this poem. Emending them away (cf. BHS) is not only an endless but a fruitless procedure, as the only determinable result is to deviate (!!) from the obvious intention of the poet to vary from the norms that he himself has established and that scholars have been at great pains to discover and isolate. [[737]] In the end it is much more rewarding and edifying to accept the text pretty much as it is and then find out just what the poet is attempting and how creative he can be in varying from expected norms and at the same time achieve a balance at the end.

When it comes to the masculine nouns, the situation is less clear, and the matching up of singular and plural may have broken down, either from the beginning, or in the course of transmission. Since the sense and force of the words are hardly affected by such shifts, the confusion between singular and plural may well be the result of transmissional variation, as the extant textual and versional evidence suggests:

1. *dābār.* This word is generally singular, but in several instances in the MT it is written and vocalized as plural: cf. vv. 57, 130, 139, 147, and 161. So in this instance, we may only speak of preponderance and a tendency to mix forms. The evidence from 11QPsalms points in the same direction.
2. *ḥōq* or *ḥuqqîm.* This word is always in the plural, although as previously noted, we have the single exceptional instance of *ḥuqqōtêkā*, which is plural, but feminine.

9. Sanders, *Dead Sea Psalms Scroll*, 46–61.

3. *mišpāṭ* and *mišpāṭîm.* Like *dābār*, this word occurs in both singular and plural forms. Here the predominance is plural, but there are six instances in the MT where the singular is used. In view of the prevalence of plural forms in the other masculine nouns, we would have to suggest that in the original intention of the poet this word should have been singular, that is if the intention was to have two singular masculine nouns and two plural masculine nouns in the poem. Unlike *dābār*, in which the singular forms predominate in the MT, here the MT has a majority of plural forms but enough singular forms to show that the situation is not clear.
4. *piqqûd* and *piqqûdîm.* This word always occurs in the masculine plural form.

We may summarize the data as follows: the feminine nouns are equally divided—two are always in the singular and the other two are predominantly if not overwhelmingly plural. The masculine nouns are less consistent. Two are always plural, while the other two are divided between singular and plural: one (*dbr*) is singular in the majority of cases, while the other (*mšpṭ*) is plural in the majority of cases. If we try to analyze or interpret the data, we find that six of the eight nouns form a pretty consistent pattern of matching singulars and plurals, certainly in the feminine, and we have two masculine nouns that are always plural. The problem arises with two masculine nouns that are inconsistent and in opposite directions. We would have to say that the schema has broken down ⟦738⟧ somewhat, and it is also not clear whether this is owing to the intention of the poet, who may have deliberately deformed or altered the original plan, or whether it resulted from scribal confusion at a point where confusion could easily happen. The question is really the extent to which the original poet may have compromised the original plan either deliberately or inadvertently. We must reckon with the notion that the poet may not always have kept every rule and principle in mind while composing what after all is a poem that has a theme and content and needed to be invented while the poet was also trying to keep all the structural devices and details under control. We will leave the question unanswered and simply record the data and possible implications. In this case, we are concerned about the mixture of singular and plural forms of *dābār* and *mišpāṭ*, both varieties of which occur in profusion throughout the Scriptures. Confusion here may have been inevitable, and the evidence of the scroll and the versions, especially the LXX, point in the direction of scribal responsibility and then an editorial tendency to normalize one form above the other (plurals predominate in the *Psalms Scroll*, while the LXX tends to preserve singular forms). While it is likely that from the beginning there was some admixture of singular and plural forms in the case of both words, the possible increase of plural forms that obscured the original intent of the balancing of masculine nouns corresponding to the feminine nouns may have resulted from scribal inattention or more conscious efforts to normalize the spelling and the forms.

Turning now to the numbers, or the frequency of occurrence of the 8 key words, we note again that there are deviations from the presumed norm of 22, that is, one instance of each key word in each stanza (as pointed out, only 3 of the 8 actually occur 22 times in the whole poem, and none of them fits the standard of one occurrence in each stanza), and that the range of deviation extends from a high of 25 in the case of *twrh* to a low of 19 in the case of *ʾmrh*. It is precisely in this pair of numbers that we find the key to the system employed by the poet. It is simply a striking example of bilateral symmetry, whereby the excess of one word (*twrh* is *three* over the norm) is balanced exactly by the deficiency of the other (*ʾmrh* is *three* under the norm); see table 2 (p. 39). Once we grasp the fact that *twrh* and *ʾmrh* form a pair, then the total of the 2 together is 25 + 19 = 44, exactly the right number for 2 key words; see table 3 (p. 40). In other words, the excess for *twrh* (the highest frequency for any word in the whole poem, which also matches the number of divine names in the poem, as already shown) is accommodated through the use of a reduced number for its companion word, *ʾmrh*. Nor is this pairing identified solely on the basis of the matching numbers, although correlating numbers would be sufficient reason in itself to reflect the intention [[739]] of the poet. As already noted, these are the only 2 words among the 8 key words that are both feminine and singular; these factors (of gender and number) also provide a clue to the thinking of the poet and serve as a guide to the rest of the pairings among the 8 key words.

There is yet one more feature that is unique to this pair, which is that together they form an envelope construction around the key-word complex, and in fact the entire poem. It will not have escaped the attentive and observant reader that the word *ʾimrâ* begins with *ʾalep* and that the word *tôrâ* begins with *taw*, the first and last letters of the Hebrew alphabet respectively. This element can hardly be accidental, because the alphabet plays such a prominent part in the whole structure of the poem. [[741]] If we are able to predicate anything about the state of mind of the poet, it is that it is saturated with notions of the alphabet, its uses and potentialities. The poet is acutely aware of the alphabetic implications and connotations in his poem: every line reflects this feature, and everything in the poem is designed not only to mirror the alphabet, but also to lead the reader into the deeper meaning and significance of its usage, in particular the notion of totality or completeness embodied in the alphabet. Just as the 22-stanza poem encompasses all the instruction of Yahweh in the religion of Israel, so the 2 key words encompass the whole list of key words and reinforce the lesson of the poem as a whole.

DISTRIBUTION OF EIGHT KEY WORDS ACCORDING TO STANZAS
SUMMARY

	1-11		12-22		TOTAL				
	Ø	2 or more	Ø	2 or more	Ø	2 or more	TOTAL	NORM	DIFF.
(1) ʾmrh	3	0	2	2	5	2	19	22	-3
(2) twrh	1	2*	0	1	1	3*	25	22	+3
	4	2	2	3	6	5*			
(3) mṣwt	1	2	2	1	3	3	22	22	0
(4) ʿdwt	2	1	1	3	3	4	23	22	+1
	3	3	3	4	6	7			
(5) dbr	2	2	1	1	3	3	22	22	0
(6) ḥqym	0	3	4	1	4	4	22	22	0
	2	5	5	2	7	7			
(7) mšpṭ	1	0	0	2	1	2	23	22	+1
(8) pqwdym	1	0	2	2	3	2	21	22	-1
	2	0	2	4	4	4			
Total	11	10*	12	13	23	23*	177	176	+1

* = ONE STANZA WITH THREE OCCURRENCES

Table 2

In my opinion, the poem not only refers directly to the Torah understood as the five books of Moses, but to the whole Hebrew Bible as then constituted, including Torah, Prophets, and Writings, a composite that also reflects an alphabetic norm for completeness.[10]

Proceeding from this first pair, we naturally look to the other two feminine nouns in the group of 8 key words for another deliberate pairing. These

10. D. N. Freedman, *The Unity of the Hebrew Bible* (Ann Arbor: University of Michigan Press, 1991).

Table 3

KEY WORD FREQUENCY I

STANZA A

	ʾmrt(k)	twrt(k)
1		① twrt yhwh
2	③ ʾmrtk	
3		② mtwrtk
4		⑤ wtwrtk
5	⑥ ʾmrtk	② twrtk
6	① kʾmrtk	④ twrtk ③ mtwrtk
7	② ʾmrtk	⑤ twrtk ⑦ twrtk
8	② kʾmrtk	⑤ twrtk ⑥ twrtk
9	③ ʾmrtk	⑧ twrt-pyk
10	④ kʾmrtk	⑤ twrtk
11	② lʾmrtk	⑤ ktwrtk
	[8] 8 k	[13] 12 k 1 o
12		④ twrtk
13	⑦ ʾmrtk	① twrtk
14		⑤ wtwrtk
15	④ kʾmrtk	① wtwrtk
16	③ wlʾmrt ṣdqk	⑥ twrtk
17	⑤ bʾmrtk	⑧ twrtk
18	④ ʾmrtk	⑥ wtwrtk
19	④ bʾmrtk	⑥ mtwrtk
20	② lʾmrtk ⑥ ʾmrtk	① twrtk
21	② ʾmrtk ② kʾmrtk	③ twrtk ⑤ twrtk
22	④ ʾmrtk	⑥ wtwrtk
	[11] 10 k 1 construct	[12] 12 k
	[19] 18 k 1 construct	[25] 24 k 1 construct

○ = STANZA LINE NUMBER

□ = TOTAL

are both found overwhelmingly if not exclusively in the plural, matching the pair that occurs exclusively in the singular (*ʾmrh* and *twrh*):

miṣwōt	22 times
ʿēdôt	23 times

In this case, the total is 45, one more than the expected total of 44, a discrepancy that needs to be investigated and discussed (table 4, p. 42). We would have expected the total to be 44 (either 22 + 22 or 21 + 23), which is the total for the remaining (masculine) pairs, as well as for the initial pair, already discussed, and therefore we should consider whether the excess in the case of either of these two words is the result of an error (presumably in scribal transmission) or a deliberate distortion or deviation on the part of the poet. It is also not beyond the realm of possibility that the poet himself was confused and lost his precise count. It is not hard to lose one's way in the intricacies of this poem, as more than one investigator has discovered to his sorrow. It is difficult to reach a decision about the intentions of a creative artist, not to speak of inadvertence, so it may be better for us to lay out the relevant data, evaluate them, and offer varying and possibly competing solutions to the dilemma.

First there are some general considerations:

(1) Of the total of 177 key words, exactly 88 are to be found in the first half of the poem (vv. 1–88), while there are 89 in the second half (vv. 89–176). If the extra word was included accidentally, we would [[743]] expect to find it in the second half of the poem rather than in the first half. This is a matter of probability, not certainty, however.

(2) Of the 176 lines in the poem, 167 have one and only one of the key words. Since these conform to the norm, it would be well to look for the anomaly or mistake among the remaining 9 lines. Four of these lines (vv. 3, 37, 90, 122) do not have any of the key words. In spite of repeated efforts on the part of scholars to supply supposedly missing words in these verses through conjectural emendation (Will Soll's misguided efforts are only the latest in the series),[11] we note that there are 2 of these "defective lines" in the first half of the poem and 2 in the second and conclude that these lines are also correct as they stand, at least in regard to the presence or absence of key words. Each of the remaining 5 lines of the poem has 2 examples of key words (vv. 16, 48, 160, 168, 172). We note again that these lines match up nicely with the 4 "defective" lines already discussed. Thus the double occurrence in the 2d stanza (v. 16) matches the omission in the 1st stanza (v. 3), and the double occurrence in the 6th stanza (v. 48) balances the omission in the 5th stanza (v. 37). The structural difficulty turns up in the second half of

11. Soll, *Psalm 119*, 155–75.

Table 4

KEY WORD FREQUENCY II

STANZA	mṣwtyk	^{c}d(w)tyk
1	(6) mṣwtyk	(2) ^{c}dtyw
2	(2) mmṣwtyk	(6) ^{c}dwtyk
3	(3) mṣwtyk (5) mmṣwtyk	(6) ^{c}dtyk (8) ^{c}dtyk
4	(8) mṣwtyk	(7) b^{c}dwtyk
5	(3) mṣwtyk	(4) ^{c}dwtyk
6	(7) bmṣwtyk (8) mṣwtyk	(6) b^{c}dtyk
7		
8	(4) mṣwtyk	(3) ^{c}dtyk
9	(2) bmṣwtyk	
10	(1) mṣwtyk	(7) ^{c}dtyk
11	(6) mṣwtyk	(8) ^{c}dwt-pyk
	[12] 12 k	[10] 9 k 1 w
12	(8) mṣwtk	(7) ^{c}dtyk
13	(2) mṣwtk	(3) ^{c}dwtyk
14		(7) ^{c}dwtyk
15	(3) mṣwt	(7) ^{c}dtyk
16	(7) mṣwtyk	(5) ^{c}dtyk
17	(3) lmṣwtyk	(1) ^{c}dwtyk
18	(7) mṣwtyk	(2) ^{c}dtyk (8) ^{c}dwtyk
19	(7) mṣwtyk	(2) ^{c}dtyk (8) m^{c}dtyk
20		(5) m^{c}dwtyk
21	(6) wmṣwtyk	(7) ^{c}dtyk (8) w^{c}dtyk
22	(4) mṣwtyk (8) mṣwtyk	
	[10] 9 k 1 o	[13] 13 k
	[22] 21 k 1 o	[23] 22 k 1 w

○ = STANZA LINE NUMBER

□ = TOTAL

the poem, where we have 3 double lines to match the 2 defective lines in the second half. On the basis of these considerations, we should therefore look at the second half of the poem and in particular at the 3 double lines in the second half (that is, the lines containing 2 of the key words) for the anomaly or discrepancy in the pattern of the poem. In other words, there should only have been 2 of these double lines to make up for the 2 defective lines in the second half of the poem, and the question then would be, whether we are able to find a clue or a reason for identifying one of the 3 double lines in the second half of the poem as the culprit (if indeed there is one).

Both of these larger considerations (and they are not unrelated) point to an excess of one key word in the second half of the poem and specifically to the 3 lines that contain 2 of the key words. We are looking particularly for examples of the 2 key words involved in this pairing: *mṣwt* and *ʿdwt*, and these words actually show up in 2 of the 3 lines: *mṣwt* in line 172 and *ʿdwt* in line 168. Neither turns up in line 160, so we may exclude that verse from further consideration. If we are looking for a possible scribal error in one of the remaining 2 lines (in this case, dittography), then we note that the word *ʿēdōtêkā* occurs in v. 167 as well as in v. 168, and that it is the 3d word in each line, so that if the poem were written stichometrically, then the word in v. 168 would be written almost directly beneath the same word in v. 167. While we cannot be sure, the ⟦744⟧ evidence from the *Psalms Scroll* from Cave 11 indicates strongly that the lines of this poem were written in just that fashion, to highlight the alphabetic character of the poem and the stanzas, so the possibility of vertical dittography (i.e., the scribe would have inadvertently copied the word from line 167 into line 168) would thereby be enhanced. In short, the best candidate for the excess word in the second half of the poem would be *wʿdtyk* in v. 168. As far as I am aware, no previous scholar has suggested this possible emendation, but it would make sense in view of the surrounding circumstances. If we were to remove it from the text, then everything would balance out in both halves of the poem: we would have the right total of 176 examples of the 8 key words; the 2 key words involved, *mṣwt* and *ʿdwt*, would occur 22 times each for a total of 44 (in the whole poem); and the 2 defective lines would be balanced by 2 overloaded lines (the former omitting any key words and the latter having 2 extra), thus matching the first half of the poem, which also has 2 defective lines and 2 overloaded lines. The totals for the feminine nouns of the poem would then be as follows:

ʾmrh	19
mṣwt	22
ʿdwt	22
twrh	25
Total	88

(2) While the proposal just made may seem attractive, even persuasive, there is yet another possibility, which at least from a text-critical point of view is even more attractive and compelling than this one. An even better candidate for vertical dittography that involves one of our 2 key words may be found in v. 48, which contains 2 key words, one of which is *mṣwtyk*. As it happens, the same word occurs in v. 47, and they occupy almost the same place in each line, as may be seen in the *Psalms Scroll* from Cave 11.[12] So the physical arrangement is almost identical to that of vv. 167–68, mentioned above, but there are two additional arguments that may be made in favor of this proposed case of vertical dittography. So strong is the hypothetical case, that many if not most scholars have proposed or accepted an emendation that would remove *mṣwtyk* (and other words) from the text of v. 48.[13] The first of these arguments [[745]] is that the dittography consists of 3 words instead of one, and this strengthens the case. Thus the text looks like this:

v. 47	b m ṣ w t y	k ʾ š r	ʾ h b t y
v. 48	m ṣ w t y	k ʾ š r	ʾ h b t y

Such an extended repetition in succeeding lines is unprecedented in the poem, and without clear indications in a different direction, I think most scholars would regard this sequence as an excellent candidate for scribal error, vertical dittography. And this is apart from the general considerations urged above. The second argument is that the duplicated words in v. 48 do not make much sense in their context. They are quite appropriate in v. 47, but in v. 48 the 3 words written above seem to be out of place and inconsistent with the preceding words, if not incoherent. As the text stands, a literal rendering of both verses would be roughly as follows:

v. 47 And I will delight myself in *your commandments, which I love*;
v. 48 And I will lift up my hands to *your commandments, which I love*;
and I will meditate on your statutes.

Long before, and quite independently of any of the general considerations that I have advanced, scholars have recommended the deletion of these three words in v. 48, chiefly on the grounds that v. 48 is much longer than v. 47, for example, or in fact longer than the normal lines in the poem, and also, as indicated above, that the sequence *wĕʾeśśāʾ-kappay ʾel-miṣwōtêkā* 'and I will lift

12. Sanders, *Psalm Scroll*, 48, Column VIII, and the plate of the entire scroll after p. 137 in the volume.

13. C. A. Briggs and E. G. Briggs, *A Critical and Exegetical Commentary on the Book of Psalms* (2 vols.; ICC; Edinburgh: T. & T. Clark, 1906–7) 2.438. H.-J. Kraus, *Psalms 60–150: A Commentary* (Continental Commentary; Minneapolis: Augsburg, 1989) 410.

up my hands to your commandments' does not make much sense. Further, in the light of Lam 3:41 (which has its own textual problems), the correct reading in Ps 119:48 should be restored as *wĕʾeśśāʾ-kappay ʾēlêkā* 'and I will lift up my hands to you. . . . ' With this emendation, the line is reduced to a more normal length, and the appropriate sense is restored in the light of the other usage (Lam 3:41). This proposal has gained wide acceptance and is regarded as virtually certain in the critical apparatus of BHS. I think there is considerable merit to this proposal and the arguments in its favor. If we were to adopt this emendation rather than the one in v. 168, then the numbers for the feminine key words would be as follows:

(1) *ʾmrh*	19	(4) *twrh*	25	=	44
(2) *mṣwt*	21	(3) *ʿdwt*	23	=	44

Certainly, this arrangement is just as symmetrical as the other proposal, and there is something especially appealing about the sequence 19, 21, [[746]] 23, 25. On the other hand, this proposal would result in a further slight disruption of the balance between the two halves of the poem, so that instead of the present 88/89 balance in the MT and the 88/88 achieved by the earlier proposal, now we would have an uneven count: 87/89. While this may not seem particularly weighty, it should be mentioned and included in the evaluation of the three different texts: the MT as we have it and the two different proposals for emending or restoring the original text. In addition, the balance between blank lines (without a key word) and double lines (with 2 key words) would be further skewed, with 2 blank lines in each half of the poem, but one double line in the first half of the poem and 3 double lines in the second half of the poem.

It is difficult to decide among the three options here: retaining the received text or going with one of the proposed emendations. Perhaps we have gone as far as it is possible to go in this matter. Whatever we decide, however, the underlying and overall pattern is clear, and the only question is how far to go with the manifest deviations, how to apportion them among the original composer and the subsequent scribes, and how to determine which variations from a supposed norm are deliberate on the part of the poet and which may be accidental or inadvertent departures, not part of the original intention.

Turning now to the masculine nouns, we may line them up as follows:

(1) *dābār*	22	(2) *ḥuqqîm*	22	=	44
(2) *mišpāṭ(îm)*	23	(4) *piqqûdîm*	21	=	44

Here there is no problem with the numbers, which are clearly right and also establish the correct pairings. The difficulty, if there is one, is that the logical

Table 5

KEY WORD FREQUENCY III

	dbr(k)	ḥqyk
1		(5) ḥqyk (8) ḥqyk
2	(1) kdbrk (8) dbrk	(4) ḥqyk (8) bḥqtyk
3	(1) dbrk	(7) bḥqyk
4	(1) kdbrk (4) kdbrk	(2) ḥqyk
5		(1) ḥqyk
6	(2) bdbrk	(8) bḥqyk
7	(1) dbr	(6) ḥqyk
8	(1) dbryk	(8) ḥqyk
9	(1) kdbrk	(4) ḥqyk (7) ḥqyk
10	(2) ldbrk	(8) bḥqyk
11	(1) ldbrk	(3) ḥqyk
	[11] 10 k, 1 o	[14] ḥqyk 13, ḥqtyk 1
12	(1) dbrk	
13	(5) dbrk	
14	(1) dbrk (3) kdbrk	(8) ḥqyk
15	(2) ldbrk	(5) bḥqyk (6) mḥqyk
16		(4) wḥqyk
17	(2) dbryk	(7) ḥqyk
18	(3) dbryk	
19	(3) ldbryk	(1) ḥqyk
20	(8) dbrk	(3) ḥqyk
21	(1) wmdbryk	
22	(1) kdbrk	(3) ḥqyk
	[11] 11 k	[8] 8 k
	[22] 21 k, 1 o	[22] 22 k

STANZA

○ = STANZA LINE NUMBER

□ = TOTAL

pairings do not follow the same pattern already determined for the feminine nouns, namely that they agree with each other in number as well as gender. For the masculine nouns, this rule does not hold, as *dābār* is predominantly singular while *ḥuqqîm* is always plural (see table 5, p. 46). Similarly, *piqqûdîm* is always plural, while *mišpāṭ* is occasionally singular (see table 6, p. 48). This crossing or mixing of singular and plural forms may reflect or be reflected in the mixture of singular and plural forms in the 2 nouns that ought to be singular throughout if the original presumed pattern of having 2 singular nouns and 2 plural nouns among the masculine forms was intended, as seems clearly to be the case with the feminine nouns. The crossover pattern of combining a singular with a plural noun to produce the required pairs may have inadvertently contributed to the origin and increase of plural forms in the singular nouns. In any case, the clear symmetrical patterns in the feminine nouns has broken down somewhat among the masculine nouns. The breakdown, if [[749]] we should call it that, is minor, however, and the larger symmetry is maintained. The number of times the 4 masculine nouns are used totals 88, which contrasts with the number of times the feminine nouns were used, which may originally have been 88 as well, but now numbers 89. The different distributions and outcomes may be tabulated as shown in tables 7 and 8 (p. 50) for the 8 key words according to gender and number.

As already noted, not one of the key words shows up in every one of the stanzas. Each one is missing in at least one of the stanzas and some in more than one (see table 9, p. 51). Given the poet's resolute control of the number and distribution of the key words in the poem, this token of incompleteness, the regularity in the pattern of omissions, is not more likely to be an inadvertence or oversight than any of the other peculiarities in the poem. Why the poet may have done this, that is, leave each key word out of at least one stanza, when more graceful and harmonious ways of correlating key words and stanzas were available to him, may be unanswerable. But the circumstance needs to be noted, as do the method and devices used by the poet to create the impression of haphazard distribution. At the same time he fit everything into the overall structure so that the parts once more come into balance and equivalence. The way in which this particular feat was accomplished was for the poet to match each blank box (the omission of a key word from a stanza) with one in which the key word or its companion occurred more than once. Beginning with the baseline number 22 (in this case 22 is the number of stanzas as well as the norm for each key word, or the double number for the pairs of key words already identified and isolated), we note that there is a necessary blank in the system for each key word that occurs fewer than the requisite number of times. Thus for the word *ʾimrâ*, which occurs only 19 times in all, there will be 3 stanzas at least in which the word cannot occur. In practice there are 5 such stanzas, but then the word itself

Table 6

KEY WORD FREQUENCY IV

STANZA

	mšpṭ(y)k	pq(w)dyk
1	(7) mšpṭy ṣdqk	(4) pqdyk
2	(5) mšpṭy-pyk	(7) bpqdyk
3	(4) mšpṭyk	
4	(6) mšpṭyk	(3) pqwdyk
5	(7) mšpṭyk	(8) lpqdyk
6	(3) lmšpṭyk	(5) pqdyk
7	(4) mšpṭyk	(8) pqdyk
8	(6) mšpṭy-ṣdqk	(7) pqwdyk
9		(5) pqwdyk
10	(3) mšpṭyk	(6) bpqwdyk
11	(4) mšpṭ	(7) pqwdyk
	[10] 9 k 1 o	[10] 10 k
12	(3) lmšpṭyk	(5) pqwdyk (6) pqwdyk
13	(6) mmšpṭyk	(4) pqwdyk (8) mpqwdyk
14	(2) mšpṭy-ṣdqk (4) mšpṭyk	(6) wmpqwdyk
15	(8) wmmšpṭyk	
16	(1) mšpṭ	(8) pqwdy-kl
17	(4) kmšpṭ	(6) pqwdyk
18	(1) mšpṭyk	(5) pqdyk
19	(5) kmšpṭk	
20	(4) kmšpṭyk (8) mšpṭ-ṣdqk	(7) pqwdyk
21	(4) mšpṭy-ṣdqk	(8) pqwdyk
22	(7) wmšpṭk	(5) pqwdyk
	[13] 11 k 2 o	[11] 11 k (?) 1 o (?)
	[23] 20 k 3 o	[21] k 21 (?)

○ = STANZA LINE NUMBER

□ = TOTAL

occurs twice in 2 of the stanzas, leaving a net deficit of 3. This means there are 5 stanzas without this word, and there are 2 with 2 occurrences of it, leaving 3 for which there is no compensatory balancing. These gaps are compensated for by the companion word *tôrâ*, which occurs 25 times and therefore has a surplus of 3 to distribute among the stanzas. In fact, the word is absent from one stanza but has multiple occurrences in 3 other stanzas, thus producing a surplus of 2 to match the deficit of 3 in the *ʾimrâ* column. We are still one short in terms of boxes, but the numerical difference is compensated for by the fact that *tôrâ* triples up in one stanza, that is, it uniquely occurs 3 times in a single stanza (see earlier discussion of the correlation between *tôrâ* and *yhwh* in this poem; both of these words occur 3 times in one [[751]] stanza, but it is a different stanza in each case). In this curious fashion, the poet is able to balance out the number of blank boxes with those that are overfilled and still reach the requisite quotas at the end. Given the unequal distribution of the key words (that is, 2 or at most 3 would [[752]] count fewer than 22 instances), there would be at least 4 or 5 blank boxes. In fact, however, the poet has expanded these to the number of 23, spread over the 8 key words and compensated by having 23 double boxes, or rather 22 double boxes and one triple box, thereby preserving the slight imbalance in the count that we noticed at the early stages of our investigation. Thus the 23 blank boxes are balanced by 23 boxes with 2 examples of key words, and it is done in such a way that the matchups are accounted for within the pairings that have already been identified. The one remaining imbalance is precisely in the pair *miṣwōt* // *ʿēdôt*, where the total is 45 occurrences rather than 44, and where we have 7 full boxes (or overfull) against 6 blank boxes. At the same time, against the 6 blank boxes in the pairing *ʾimrâ* // *tôrâ*, we have, as already noted, only 5 full boxes (with 2 occurrences each), except that the deficit is made up for by having a third instance of *tôrâ* to match up with the deficit on the other side. The end result is that we have the same number of boxes on both sides: 23 blanks and 23 filled, but the actual numbers vary by one. There are 24 examples in the 23 full boxes to over-balance the 23 blank boxes. What this seems to show is that the imbalance is integral to the poem, rather than being the result of scribal error, and that the poet has been coping with this structural assymmetry from the beginning and has incorporated it into the structure of the poem. Since the procedure in the case of these blank and filled boxes does not affect and is not affected by the other mismatches, the conclusion would seem to be that all, or nearly all, of the apparent distortions are inherent in the original structure and are not the result of subsequent aberrations.

The number of blank boxes for each word ranges from one (a single omission in the 22 stanzas, as in the case of *twrh* and *mšpṭ*) to 5 (in the case of *ʾmrh*). In most instances, the apparent loss is made up by double boxes for

DISTRIBUTION OF EIGHT KEY WORDS ACCORDING TO GENDER

	MT			EMENDATION I			EMENDATION II		
Feminine Nouns	1-11	12-22	T	1-11	12-22	T	1-11	12-22	T
(1) ᵓmrh	8	11	19	8	11	19	8	11	19
(2) mṣwt	12	10	22	*11	10	21	12	10	22
(3) ᶜdwt	10	13	23	10	13	23	10	*12	22
(4) twrh	13	12	25	13	12	25	13	12	25
Total	43	46	89	42	46	88	43	45	88
Masculine Nouns									
(1) dbr	11	11	22	11	11	22	11	11	22
(2) ḥqym	14	8	22	14	8	22	14	8	22
(3) mšpṭ	10	13	23	10	13	23	10	13	23
(4) pqwdym	10	11	21	10	11	21	10	11	21
Total	45	43	88	45	43	88	45	43	88
Totals	88	89	177	87	89	176	88	88	176

* = EMENDATION

Table 7

DISTRIBUTION OF EIGHT KEY WORDS ACCORDING TO NUMBER

	MT			EMENDATION I			EMENDATION II		
Singular Nouns	1-11	12-22	T	1-11	12-22	T	1-11	12-22	T
(1) ᵓmrh	8	11	19	8	11	19	8	11	19
(2) twrh	13	12	25	13	12	25	13	12	25
(3) dbr	11	11	22	11	11	22	11	11	22
(4) mšpṭ	10	13	23	10	13	23	10	13	23
Total	42	47	89	42	47	89	42	47	89
Plural Nouns									
(1) mṣwt	12	10	22	*11	10	21	12	10	22
(2) ᶜdwt	10	13	23	10	13	23	10	*12	22
(3) ḥqym	14	8	22	14	8	22	14	8	22
(4) pqwdym	10	11	21	10	11	21	10	11	21
Total	46	42	88	45	42	87	46	41	87
Totals	88	89	177	87	89	176	88	88	176

*** = EMENDATION**

Table 8

KEY WORD OCCURRENCES

Line (*Verse*)

STANZA

	ᵓmrh	dbr	ḥqym	mṣwt	mšpt	ᶜdwt	pqwdym	twrh	Total
I			5 *(5)*, 8 *(8)*	6 *(6)*	7 *(7)*	2 *(2)*	4 *(4)*	1 *(1)*	***7*** 6 (2)
II	3 *(19)*	1 *(9)*, 8 *(16)*	4 *(12)*, 8 *(16)*	2 *(10)*	5 *(13)*	6 *(14)*	7 *(15)*		***9*** 7 (1)
III		1 *(17)*	7 *(23)*	3 *(19)*, 5 *(21)*	4 *(20)*	6 *(22)*, 8 *(24)*		2 *(18)*	***8*** 6 (2)
IV		1 *(25)*, 4 *(28)*	2 *(26)*	8 *(32)*	6 *(30)*	7 *(31)*	3 *(27)*	5 *(29)*	***8*** 7 (1)
V	6 *(38)*		1 *(33)*	3 *(35)*	7 *(39)*	4 *(36)*	8 *(40)*	2 *(34)*	***7*** 7 (1)
VI	1 *(41)*	2 *(42)*	8 *(40)*	7 *(47)*, 8 *(48)*	3 *(43)*	6 *(46)*	5 *(45)*	4 *(44)*	***9*** 8 (0)
VII	2 *(50)*	1 *(49)*	6 *(54)*		4 *(52)*		8 *(56)*	3 *(51)*, 5 *(53)*, 7 *(55)*	***8*** 6 (2)
VIII	2 *(58)*	1 *(57)*	8 *(64)*	4 *(60)*	6 *(62)*	3 *(59)*	7 *(63)*	5 *(61)*	***8*** 8 (0)
IX	3 *(67)*	1 *(65)*	4 *(68)*, 7 *(71)*	2 *(66)*			5 *(69)*	6 *(70)*, 8 *(72)*	***8*** 6 (2)
X	4 *(76)*	2 *(74)*	8 *(80)*	1 *(73)*	3 *(75)*	7 *(79)*	6 *(78)*	5 *(77)*	***8*** 8 (0)
XI	2 *(82)*	1 *(81)*	3 *(83)*	6 *(86)*	4 *(84)*	8 *(88)*	7 *(87)*	5 *(85)*	***8*** 8 (0)
Subtotal	8 8 (3) / 0	11 9 (2) / 2	14 11 (0) / 3	12 10 (1) / 2	10 10 (1) / 0	10 9 (2) / 1	10 10 (1) / 0	13 10 (1) / 3	***88*** 77(11)
XII		1 *(89)*		8 *(96)*	3 *(91)*	7 *(95)*	5 *(93)*, 6 *(94)*	4 *(92)*	***7*** 6 (2)
XIII	7 *(103)*	5 *(101)*		2 *(98)*	6 *(102)*	3 *(99)*	4 *(100)*, 8 *(104)*	1 *(97)*	***8*** 7 (1)
XIV		1 *(105)*, 3 *(107)*	8 *(112)*		2 *(106)*, 4 *(108)*	7 *(111)*	6 *(110)*	5 *(109)*	***8*** 6 (2)
XV	4 *(116)*	2 *(114)*	5 *(117)*, 6 *(118)*	3 *(115)*	8 *(120)*	7 *(119)*		1 *(113)*	***8*** 7 (1)
XVI	3 *(123)*		4 *(124)*	7 *(127)*	1 *(121)*	5 *(125)*	8 *(128)*	6 *(126)*	***7*** 7 (1)
XVII	5 *(133)*	2 *(130)*	7 *(135)*	3 *(131)*	4 *(132)*	1 *(129)*	6 *(134)*	8 *(136)*	***8*** 8 (0)
XVIII	4 *(140)*	3 *(139)*		7 *(143)*	1 *(137)*	2 *(138)*, 8 *(144)*	5 *(141)*	6 *(142)*	***8*** 7 (1)
XIX	4 *(148)*	3 *(147)*	1 *(145)*	7 *(151)*	5 *(149)*	2 *(146)*, 8 *(152)*		6 *(150)*	***8*** 7 (1)
XX	2 *(154)*, 6 *(158)*	8 *(160)*	3 *(155)*		4 *(156)*, 8 *(160)*	5 *(157)*	7 *(159)*	1 *(153)*	***9*** 7 (1)
XXI	2 *(162)*	1 *(161)*		6 *(166)*	4 *(164)*	7 *(167)*, 8 *(168)*	8 *(168)*	3 *(163)*, 5 *(165)*	***9*** 7 (1)
XXII	2 *(170)*, 4 *(172)*	1 *(169)*	3 *(171)*	4 *(172)*, 8 *(176)*	7 *(175)*		5 *(173)*	6 *(174)*	***9*** 7 (1)
Subtotal	11 9 (2) / 2	11 10 (1) / 1	8 7 (4) / 1	10 9 (2) / 1	13 11 (0) / 2	13 10 (1) / 3	11 9 (2) / 2	12 11 (0) / 1	***89*** 76(12)

KEY TO SUBTOTAL BOXES

Total occurrences

Stanzas with key word (Without key word) / Key word appears more than once

KEY TO TOTAL COLUMN

Occurrences

Key words (Key words omitted)

Table 9

the same word or its companion, and the variation is minimal when it comes to the word itself or the pair. The major deviation comes with the pair already cited, *ᵓmrh* and *twrh*, where *ᵓmrh* has a net deficit of 3, while *twrh* has a net surplus of 3, but it is compressed into 2 boxes, instead of the

KEY WORDS SUMMARY BY STANZA

LINE NUMBERS

	1	2	3	4	5	6	7	8	
I	twrh	ʿdwt		pqwdym	ḥqym	mṣwt	mšpṭ	ḥqym	7
II	dbr	mṣwt	ʾmrh	ḥqym	mšpṭ	ʿdwt	pqwdym	dbr ḥq	9
III	dbr	twrh	mṣwt	mšpṭ	mṣwt,	ʿdwt	ḥqym	ʿdwt	8
IV	dbr	ḥqym	pqwdym	dbr	twrh	mšpṭ	ʿdwt	mṣwt	8
V	ḥqym	twrh	mṣwt	ʿdwt		ʾmrh	mšpṭ	pqwdym	7
VI	ʾmrh	dbr	mšpṭ	twrh	pqwdym	ʿdwt	mṣwt	mṣwt ḥqym	*9
VII	dbr	ʾmrh	twrh	mšpṭ	twrh	ḥqym	twrh	pqwdym	8
VIII	dbr	ʾmrh	ʿdwt	mṣwt	twrh	mšpṭ	pqwdym	ḥqym	*8
IX	dbr	mṣwt	ʾmrh	ḥqym	pqwdym	twrh	ḥqym	twrh	8
X	mṣwt	dbr	mšpṭ	ʾmrh	twrh	pqwdym	ʿdwt	ḥqym	*8
XI	dbr	ʾmrh	ḥqym	mšpṭ	twrh	mṣwt	pqwdym	ʿdwt	*8
	11	11	10	11	10	11	11	13	88
XII	dbr		mšpṭ	twrh	pqwdym	pqwdym	ʿdwt	mṣwt	7
XIII	twrh	mṣwt	ʿdwt	pqwdym	dbr	mšpṭ	ʾmrh	pqwdym	8
XIV	dbr	mšpṭ	dbr	mšpṭ	twrh	pqwdym	ʿdwt	ḥqym	8
XV	twrh	dbr	mṣwt	ʾmrh	ḥqym	ḥqym	ʿdwt	mšpṭ	8
XVI	mšpṭ		ʾmrh	ḥqym	ʿdwt	twrh	mṣwt	pqwdym	7
XVII	ʿdwt	dbr	mṣwt	mšpṭ	ʾmrh	pqwdym	ḥqym	twrh	*8
XVIII	mšpṭ	ʿdwt	dbr	ʾmrh	pqwdym	twrh	mṣwt	ʿdwt	8
XIX	ḥqym	ʿdwt	dbr	ʾmrh	mšpṭ	twrh	mṣwt	ʿdwt	8
XX	twrh	ʾmrh	ḥqym	mšpṭ	ʿdwt	ʾmrh	pqwdym	dbr mšpṭ	9
XXI	dbr	ʾmrh	twrh	mšpṭ	twrh	mṣwt	ʿdwt	ʿdwt pqwdym	9
XXII	dbr	ʾmrh	ḥqym	ʾmrh mṣwt	pqwdym	twrh	mšpṭ	mṣwt	9
	11	9	11	12	11	11	11	13	89
	22	20	21	23	21	22	22	26	177

* = STANZAS WITH EVERY KEY WORD

Table 10

expected 3. The result for this pair is that the number of key words is made up exactly, but there is a discrepancy in the number of boxes, namely, 6 blanks and 6 words but only 5 filled boxes. This in turn balances out with the pair *mṣwt* // *ʿdwt*, where there are 6 blank boxes matched by 7 full ones. Adding these pairs together (the group of feminine nouns already discussed at some length) we come up with 12 blank boxes and 12 full boxes, but the latter are slightly overfilled, since they contain 13 words rather than the expected 12. The masculine nouns in this case are quite regular, with each pair balancing out exactly: the pair [[753]] *dbr // ḥqym* comes out at 7 and 7, while the other pair *mšpṭ // pqwdym* are also all even at 4 and 4. The totals: 12//12 and 11//11 come out even at 23, with the qualification already noted for the feminine nouns. Finally, the number 23 cannot be separated from the alphabetic pattern either, although it is less common, in comparison with the usual number 22. Thus everything balances out, or would, with 23 blank boxes and 23 filled ones, except for the third *twrh* in stanza 7 (lines 49–56), which also produces the extra key word for the poem, although it is a different word in a different place from the ones that we have been considering for this distinction. All this implies that everything we have in the text somehow belongs where it is, although it is always possible that in the midst of these complications and intricacies, the poet himself had difficulty finding his way and keeping track of all the details, and he may have wondered what to do about a few loose threads and untidy borders.

Now, before winding up the paper, I would like to look once again at the stanzas and once again find a basic uniformity along with a great deal of variation and diversity in detail, always within the boundaries of the main framework of the poem. Let us remind ourselves that the ideal or normative pattern would produce stanzas in which one key word would appear in each line, and that all 8 would show up in each stanza. While this pattern would impose rather strict regularity on the poem, it would allow for considerable variation in the order in which the key words turn up: they would not have to appear in the same order in each stanza, and while some of them tend to appear in particular lines of each stanza, overall there is no discernible pattern in the order of the key words. When it comes to the actual situation, not only are no two stanzas the same, but there is considerable variation from this presumed norm, some major departures and always minor ones.

First of all, only 4 out of 22 stanzas conform to the basic pattern we have proposed: stanzas in which each of the 8 key words appears only once and each one in a different line (cf. stanzas 8, 10, 11, 17); see table 10 (p. 52). As already indicated, the order in which the key words appear is not the same in any of them, although there are some correspondences in placement. There is one other stanza that has the 8 key words distributed one per line through the stanza, but it also has a 9th key word that doubles up with one of the others in the last line of the stanza, so it must be regarded as a variant from the basic pattern. Actually, this occurs in stanza 6, where *mṣwtyk* in line 48 (the 8th line of the stanza) is not only one of two key words in the line, but also duplicates *mṣwtyk*, immediately above it in line 47. (See the earlier discussion, pp. 44–47.) This circumstance might be regarded as another argument in favor of emending the second *mṣwtyk* out of the text and thus restoring a stanza that [[754]] conforms much better to the ideal pattern, but the fact that most of the stanzas do not conform to this pattern suggests that the argument may be less than compelling.

Second, all the rest of the stanzas omit at least one of the key words, and some omit more than one, but never more than 2:

Category	*Stanzas 1–11*		*Stanzas 12–22*		*Total*
Omit None	6, 8, 10, 11	(4)	17	(1)	5
Omit One	2, 4, 5	(3)	13, 15, 16, 18, 19, 20, 21, 22	(8)	11
Omit Two	1, 3, 7, 9	(4)	12, 14	(2)	6
Total		11		11	22

[[755]] What emerges from the tabulation is the impression that the normal stanza is one that omits one of the key words, and that the unusual arrangements are those in which all the key words are included or those in which two of the key words are omitted. The latter two categories tend to balance each other out, a phenomenon we have noted throughout the study.

When it comes to the number of key words per stanza, the range is relatively small, from a minimum of 7 to a maximum of 9, very close to the normative figure of 8, which also predominates:

Number of Key Words per Stanza	*Stanzas 1–11*		*Stanzas 12–22*		*Total*
7	1, 5	(2)	12, 16	(2)	4
8	3, 4, 7, 8, 9, 10, 11	(7)	13, 14, 15, 17, 18, 19	(6)	13
9	2, 6	(2)	20, 21, 22	(3)	5

While the number 8 is dominant, the distribution is uneven, with only 4 of the 13 instances having 8 different key words. The stanzas with only 7 key words are balanced by those with 9, almost exactly. The over-balance (in the second half of the poem) derives from one of the places where there is a suspected dittography (line 168, stanza 21).

We may sum up the findings thus far in the following way: there is a simple basic pattern or structure in this poem, which begins with the alphabet (in an acrostic pattern) and a fixed 8-line stanza and then is extended to include 8 key words that form the basic internal structure of the poem. While the overall number of these words is carefully controlled (an actual total of 177 compared with the normative or expected 176), there is extensive variation in the distribution and arrangement of these words in the poem itself. This widespread variety is the deliberate [[756]] expression of the poet's creativity and ingenuity in maintaining the overall structure of the poem while also indulging in pyrotechnics of different kinds, a dazzling display of virtuosity in handling technical matters of intricacy and complexity, while at the same time conveying a profound religious message.

Chapter 3

The Structure of Psalm 119: Part II

DAVID NOEL FREEDMAN

[[55]] This paper is the continuation and completion of an earlier presentation on the structure of Psalm 119. The first part dealt mainly with the acrostic pattern of the poem as a whole, and the number and distribution of key-words in it (Freedman, [1995][1]). This part will deal with questions of quantity and meter in this poem, along with other related matters.

Before turning to these, however, I wish to consider two textual problems not treated in the former paper that may have some bearing on the metrical analysis below, since they are sufficiently problematic to warrant possible emendation of MT. In both cases we have alternate readings in the 11Q Psalm Scroll (11QPs[a]) and the LXX whose evidence, while not identical in either case, tends to support a reading that may well be more original and superior to that in MT.

(1) In v. 49, MT reads *zĕkōr dābār,* while 11QPs[a] has *zkwrh dbrykh* and LXX has *mnēsthēti ton logon sou,* reflecting a Hebrew *Vorlage*: *zĕkōr dĕbārekā.* It seems likely that LXX preserves the original reading of the key-word *dābār,* that is, the singular noun with the second m.s. suffix; MT apparently has lost the suffix, while 11QPs[a] modified the singular noun to a plural. LXX and 11QPs[a] agree in representing the pronominal suffix omitted in MT. In the whole poem, this is the only instance in which the key-word *dābār* lacks the suffix in MT. The argument is not decisive, and this may be a deliberate exception to the pattern, but the preponderance of the evidence points to the reading of LXX and 11Ps[a].

Reprinted, with permission, from *Biblical and Other Studies in Honor of Reuben Ahroni on the Occasion of His Sixtieth Birthday* (ed. T. J. Lewis) = *Hebrew Annual Review* 14 (1994) 55–87. Original pagination is marked by page number in [[ ]].

1. Elucidation of the poem's structure, as well as references to other works, may be found there.

⟦56⟧ (2) In v. 128, MT has an extremely awkward reading: *ʿal-kēn kol piqqûdê kōl yiššartî.* The repetition of the word *kōl* is difficult to explain or justify. At this point, 11QPs[a] offers a better text, *ʿl kn pqwdy kwl yšrty*, but it still lacks coherence. LXX has the best reading of all: *dia toûto pros pasas tas entolas sou katōrthoumēn*, reflecting a Hebrew *Vorlage* of *ʿal-kēn lĕkol-piqqûdêkā yiššartî.* Certainly, this is the most understandable text, and in all likelihood the second *kōl* of MT was originally the second m.s. suffix. Whether or not we need to restore the preposition *lĕ* before *kol-piqqûdêkā* is moot in the light of frequent ellipsis in Hebrew poetry.

Nevertheless, in order to avoid even the appearance of adjusting the text to fit metrical theories or presumed requirements, we will follow MT throughout the following treatment of the text, and restrict ourselves to recording possible alternate syllable-counts in cases like the two just cited. Any differences will be slight, almost invisible in the framework of the whole poem, and well within any margin of error or variation that we must allow in dealing with Hebrew poetry generally and with such a lengthy poem in particular.

Regarding the metrical structure of the poem, we begin with a quotation from the Church father and historian Eusebius of Caesarea, who writes in the *Praeparatio Evangelica*, xi.5.5:

> There would also be found among them poems in metre, like the great song of Moses and David's 118th Psalm, composed in what the Greeks call heroic metre. At least it is said (*phasi goun*) that these are hexameters, consisting of sixteen syllables; also their other compositions in verse are said to consist of trimeter and tetrameter lines according to the sound of their own language.

So far as I am aware, this is the only statement from antiquity about biblical Hebrew poetry in which the number of syllables in a Hebrew verse or line is specified: sixteen for the lines in the Song of Moses (Deut 32:1–43) and the Great Psalm (Psalm 119 in MT, 118 in LXX). The primary purpose of the present inquiry is to test the statement by Eusebius and determine whether or not the lines of Psalm 119 have sixteen syllables each, as Eusebius states (I intend to examine this feature of Deuteronomy 32 elsewhere). Since even a cursory examination of the MT shows that the statement cannot be precisely true without extensive emendation, is there yet any sense in which the statement might be true? If there is some significant correspondence between the statement in Eusebius' work and the text that has come down to us (or as preserved in 11QPs[a] or reflected in LXX), then Eusebius becomes an important witness to a long-standing tradition concerning Hebrew poetry, and to the ⟦57⟧ fact that the Hebrews did count syllables, after all, like poets in the western Indo-European tradition, and not just accented syllables. It is understood that Eusebius' statement may only reflect circumstances in his own day (4th century C.E.). Because the pronunciation of biblical Hebrew at that time was not the same as in the first millennium B.C.E., Eusebius' observation may not reflect accurately the metrical particulars at the time of composition or first liturgical usage.

Whether or not Eusebius was aware of possible changes in the pronunciation of Biblical Hebrew during the post-biblical centuries, he intended his remarks to apply to the time of composition and first usage. We will test the hypothesis by restoring and reconstructing biblical Hebrew of the classical period, specifically for the Second Temple (about the 5th century B.C.E.) when Psalm 119 may have been composed and used. Although we rely upon MT, its text and vocalization, for the pronunciation of biblical Hebrew (and therefore for the syllable count), we are reasonably sure that MT incorporates certain subsequent alterations and modifications in pronunciation that affect the counting of syllables. The differences are for the most part rather slight, but if we are to be as accurate as possible and maintain control over the numbers, then this procedure can hardly be avoided. Thus, it is commonly agreed among scholars that such phenomena as *pataḥ-furtive* and helping vowels associated with laryngeals (e.g., *yaʿăleh* for an older *yaʿleh*) are secondary and were introduced long after the biblical period, and therefore they should not be retained when reconstructing Classical Hebrew. Similarly, it is recognized that two-syllable segholate formations, such as *melek* or *šaʿar*, were originally monosyllabic (*malk* and *šaʿr*) and should be treated as one syllable.[2] In addition to the tendency in MT to add syllables, there are contrary tendencies to contract words and syllables, and some of these practices also seem to be later than the classical period. Thus, the reduction of short vowels to vocal *shewa* does not mean that they should then be left out of the count, as though there were no difference between vocal and silent *shewa* (as some modern scholars seem to think). The question of [[58]] vowel-length, and therefore syllable-length, is very difficult, and it does not seem possible or feasible to deal adequately with this phenomenon. I have made some strenuous attempts at accommodating differences in length of syllables, but there remains considerable uncertainty about many of the syllables. Although I am certain that the Hebrew did make distinctions between long and short syllables (particularly significant for poetry), at this stage of the inquiry we will be content merely

2. Where MT lengthens or extends the pronunciation of a word, it is less likely to reflect actual usage in antiquity, and in most such cases we ignore the datum. The same is true of the resolution of diphthongs into two-syllable combinations (e.g., *mayim* for an older *maym*, or *mawet* derived from diphthongal *mawt*. The traditional explanation is that such expansions and extensions were designed by the Masoretes (or the Rabbis behind them) to ensure the proper Hebrew pronunciation of these words, which was in danger of being contaminated by the prevailing Aramaic pronunciation of the general population. Regardless of the reasoning, these are demonstrably secondary developments in Masoretic Hebrew.

to count syllables without regard to syllable length. For the present, we will simply assume that in large units and over whole poems, the long and short (with the very long and very short) vowels and syllables balance out, so that the numbers will correspond on the two sides of any equation. In the end, both the claims and the tests will be limited to the numbers. While Eusebius and others (like Josephus, Origen, and Jerome) made extensive use of analogies with Greek poetry especially, in the end Eusebius settled for a number: sixteen syllables for the lines or verses of Hebrew poetry as exemplified in the Song of Moses and the Great Psalm. We will settle for the same rather crude but specific number: sixteen syllables per line.

I will concede at once that absolute precision is impossible under any circumstances, so I wish to allow for a certain range of possibility in the syllable-counts. The target will lie somewhere between the boundaries established by the lowest and highest counts for lines, stanzas, and whole poems. We can thus accommodate our own uncertainty in various instances as to the exact pronunciation (and therefore the number of syllables) and also allow for flexibility on the part of the poet and even general usage among poets of that time. Concerning the latter, it is well known that English language poets (and presumably this is true of other language groups) exercise considerable flexibility and freedom in making words fit the meter of their poems. Words are often shortened or lengthened, syllables are eliminated or added, so that the lines conform to the underlying pattern of the poetry. Although we will not exercise that freedom at all in dealing with Hebrew poetry, we can assume that it existed, and that in practice the poets achieved greater conformity to their basic patterns than we can ever reproduce. In other words, what we have to regard as departure or deviation from the norms may have been thought of as a small measure of poetic license and well within the general guidelines for poets of that age.

While we will take the words as we find them, we will also allow for different possible vocalizations or pronunciations. The second m.s. pronominal suffix is all but ubiquitous in the poem, occurring about 225 times in a poem of 176 lines or verses. In MT this suffix is always written with a [[59]] simple final *kap*, while in 11QPs[a] it is always written with a final *heh* (כה-). Curiously, in almost every case, MT vocalizes the final *kap* as though it were written כה-, i.e., *-kā* rather than *-āk* or *-ēk* (which occurs twice).[3] The Masoretes usually followed the consonantal spelling tradition preserved in the great medieval codices (e.g., Aleppo and Leningrad) and vocalized the text in most cases in conformity with the indications and implications of the standard biblical text. Exceptionally, in the case of the second m.s. pronominal suffix (and

3. These two forms are both suffixed to the same preposition: *lāk* (vv. 11 and 62; cf. *lĕkā* in v. 94).

a few other cases, e.g., second m.s. verbal forms, and third f.s. pronominal forms) they followed another tradition, which may be reflected in the different spelling practices of the Qumran community. The Masoretes apparently believed that the longer pronunciation of the second m.s. suffixes had greater claim to validity than the shorter form reflected in the preferred spelling. At the same time, they clearly recognized that the shorter spelling was acceptable in certain circumstances in biblical Hebrew (e.g., in pausal position).[4] Our problem is how to determine which vocalization the poet himself used and what he intended when he composed the poem. The short form has been generalized through the consonantal spelling of the manuscripts, while the Masoretes have preserved the longer form in their vocalization of the text. The Masoretic vocalization is rooted in oral tradition and transmission, and if the longer form is more original, then MT in its vocalization may well reflect the actual usage of the poet. The poet himself may well have used both forms under different circumstances, it now being impossible to tell what determined the selection of either in any given locus. We now have inscriptional evidence from the First Temple period showing that both long and short forms were in use concurrently. Therefore, we will give both counts, the long and the short in the case of all of these ambiguous forms, providing thereby a minimum and a maximum count for the poem, line by line and as a whole. We can then presume that the actual accurate count for the lines and the poem lies somewhere between the lower and the higher numbers.

The vocalization of the second m.s. form of the perfect verb is similarly problematic. All seven verbs in the poem with the second m.s. form of the perfect are vocalized with the ending *-tā*, but only one is spelled out in the [[60]] test with the final *heh* (*ṣwyth*, v. 4). The other six are spelled defectively, with nothing after the final *taw*. While the Masoretes employed a uniform vocalization, the actual spelling in MT (here and elsewhere in the Hebrew Bible) shows that there were two different forms of the verb, one spelled תה- and pronounced *-tâ*, the other spelled ת- and presumably pronounced *-t* (with no final vowel). The actual pronunciation reflected, and was reflected in, the spelling. When the word is spelled in full, there is no question about the vocalization or the corresponding syllable-count. But when the form is mixed with the short spelling and the long vocalization (as in the six other cases in MT of Psalm 119), then we cannot decide the matter and will give both counts, the low and the high.

Finally, we must consider two other classes of variation in counting syllables. In these instances MT presents contractions of normal forms, a

4. See the pausal form *lāk* in Ps 119:11, 62 (cf. *lĕkā* in v. 94). The distinction in MT seems artificial, and I do not think that the short form was actually limited to the pausal position. I believe that is was more widespread, but less common than the long form.

reduced count where originally there was an additional syllable in a word or combination with a preposition. We cannot be certain when such contractions took place in the history of the language, and so we include both counts in our reckoning. Most instances occur when prepositions are attached to following nouns, whether verbal (e.g., *lĕ* + infinitive construct) or substantival. Thus in the case of *lišmōr*, MT has two syllables, whereas originally there were probably three syllables: *lĕ* + the two-syllable infinitive of the regular verb. Similarly in a phrase like *kid*(*ĕ*)*bar*, scholars used to speak of half-open syllables and debated whether the *shewa* should be pronounced or not. Originally, we may assume that there were three syllables in such a combination, but MT probably reflects a contraction to two syllables (cf. *bid*(*ĕ*)*rākāyw* in v. 3, which should be counted as having had originally four syllables but in MT seems to have three). One may say in such instances that there is a minimum and a maximum count: three or at most four syllables. The problem is whether such contractions took place in biblical times, and if they did, when. Because one cannot give a definitive answer, it is better to retain the ambiguity and include such cases in both of our counts. If may well be that the poets of biblical antiquity could and did exercise some freedom on their own in using contractions, while the uncontracted forms remained in use in another sector of the Hebrew-speaking population (e.g., such forms as "ne'er" and "e'en" in English poetry did not displace the normal uncontracted forms "never" and "even"). We have counted 31 instances of such contractions in Psalm 119, and all are included in our double-counting system.

In the second of the two final classes of variation mentioned above, there is one clear example in v. 41 of an initial conjunctive *wĕ* attached to a word with the *shewa* merged into the following vowel, resulting in the loss of a [[61]] syllable: *wîbōʾūnî* (four syllables). Originally there was an additional syllable in this complex, but because it is difficult to tell whether the contraction took place in biblical times, we include both counts, short and long. In other words, when MT introduces a contraction in the text, it may reflect an authentic development in the language, or the usage of the poet, and we wish to recognize that possibility.

As soon as we begin to test the statement from Eusebius about sixteen-syllable lines in this Great Psalm, we run into a problem. The first line barely passes:

ʾašrê tĕmîmê-dārek hahōlĕkîm bĕtôrat yahweh

Syllable count:	2 + 3 + 1/2	= 6/7
	4 + 3 + 2	= 9

If we follow MT exactly, we have a total of 16, but it is not likely that the word *dārek* was so pronounced in biblical times; the evidence points strongly to a monosyllable **dark*. Nevertheless, the total of 15 (or 16) is close to the standard and one can proceed to the next line or verse:

ʾašrê nōṣĕrê ʿēdōtāyw bĕkol-lēb yidrĕšûhû

Syllable count:	2 + 3 + 3	= 8
	2 + 1 + 4	= 7

Here the total of 15 is unambiguous, again close but not exactly the prescribed 16. By the third verse, it is unmistakably clear that there is a problem in assessing the Eusebian statement about this poem:

ʾap lōʾ-pāʿălû ʿawlâ   bidĕrākāyw hālākû

Syllable count:	1 + 1 + 3 + 2	= 7
	3/4 + 3	= 6/7

Here the total of 13/14 is substantially less than the standard of 16 specified by Eusebius. As we have seen, not one of these lines is clearly or certainly sixteen syllables long, and one of them is distinctively shorter. When we examine the remaining lines in the poem, the same pattern of nonconformity to a specific pattern will hold. Not all of the lines will be shorter than the [[62]] norm. Some will be longer, some shorter, and some will be exactly sixteen syllables long.

The initial impression is that the distribution is random, and one can construct a bell-shaped curve to represent the actual syllable-counts per line and their frequencies. In any case, while there may be some difference of opinion among scholars as to the exact count in each case, regardless of the system used, the result will be in conflict with Eusebius' statement taken at face value. The fact is that the lines of the poem are not each sixteen syllables long. We cannot even say that the great bulk of the lines are sixteen syllables long, nor that that is the predominant number in counting the syllables of the lines of the poem. In an English sonnet, each line is supposed to be ten syllables long. Not all of them may be, for a variety of reasons, but the great majority will be, and the remainder will rarely differ from the norm by more than one syllable. That is not the case with this psalm, or with poems generally in the Bible that have a similar structure. Furthermore, in the case of this poem (and Lamentations 3), each line is carefully demarked and delimited by the use of the alphabetic acrostic feature, so there is no question as to line length and boundaries. While individual lines may be defective or excessive, owing to scribal mistransmission, the poem as a whole is substantially intact. Variations in line length cannot be regarded as a distortion or a disfigurement of the original metrically perfect poem. Given that the number and length of the lines are predetermined, there can be no challenge to the initial conclusion that the lines are not each sixteen syllables long, as Eusebius seems to suggest. The only way a result could be achieved to conform to the statement in Eusebius would be by extensive emendations of the text, by regarding many of the lines as defective (too short) or excessive (too long), and by adding and subtracting words and phrases to achieve the kind of uniformity that may be implied in the statement.

Unless we are disposed (as G. B. Gray was [1972: pp. 12–13]) to dismiss the statement as meaningless or irrelevant, we must interpret it in a different fashion. One can also understand Eusebius to mean that the number of syllables is a norm or average for the poem as a whole, calculated by dividing the total number of syllables in the entire poem by the number of lines (176). We contend that the poet achieved this result by consciously adopting and consistently applying a system of compensation, whereby shorter lines were balanced by longer lines, so that the correct total number, and thereby the average, were reached in this manner. We have already seen this process at work in the much more complicated task of counting and distributing keywords throughout the poem, so it is quite reasonable and in fact easier to [[63]] apply the same principles and procedures in the case of syllable-counting. The key number, therefore, is not to have sixteen syllables for each line, but 16 × 176 (lines) = 2,816 for the poem as a whole.

We now summarize the findings of such an analysis. There are 263 instances in Psalm 119 (MT) in which there is sufficient ambiguity to justify a short count and a long count. These may be categorized as follows:

2. The pronominal suffix of the second m.s. person:	225
3. The pronominal suffix of perfect verbs:	6
4. Prepositions attached to nouns:	31
5. The conjunction *wĕ* attached to verb:	1
Total:	263

If one takes these cases into consideration in counting all of the syllables in the poem, the result is the following range in the total count: long count 2,902; short count 2,639.

The correct syllable count for the poem as a whole is somewhere between the low and high numbers just given. In the same way one can determine a range for the average number of syllables per line in the poem. Thus, in adopting the low count, one is very close to an average number of fifteen syllables per line (the total would be 2,640 for the poem, whereas our lowest possible count is 2,639). The average for the high count is close to sixteen and a half syllables. If one takes into account the evidence from other poems in the Bible, especially those with an alphabetic acrostic structure (where the line count and boundaries are indisputable) or with the same kind of structure without the alphabetic device, the results are very similar: a spread from fifteen to seventeen syllables for the average line or bicolon. And where the spread is smaller than in the present instance (where the continual recurrence of the second m.s. pronominal suffix is a special feature of the psalm), the average tends to be even close to the pivotal number sixteen. In this way we return to the statement by Eusebius with which the discussion began. If his statement is interpreted to mean that the "average line" of Hebrew poetry, as seen in the Great Psalm (119), consisted of sixteen syllables, then the statement can be confirmed, for within a certain range, the number sixteen is certainly represented. If the number sixteen is assigned as the average line length for this poem, there would be a total of 2,816 syllables, which is well [[64]] within the range determined by other means. There is reason to believe that Eusebius was citing an authentic tradition about biblical Hebrew poetry when he mentioned this number, and that the ancient poet was governed or at least guided by a numerical consideration in the composition of this work. Furthermore, the number applies to many, many more poems than Eusebius listed, and may be regarded as the standard for much of biblical poetry: the typical bicolon in books such as Psalms, Proverbs, and Job has an average line length of sixteen syllables, and there are many other poems throughout the Bible that share the same general format.

In Psalm 119, the extensive use of the second m.s. pronominal suffix has precluded the possibility of exactitude in making this numerical determination, but given the propensity and predilection for precision, especially in symmetrical balancing, one may plausibly infer that the actual syllable count for the poem when composed was very close to the norm established above: 2,816. Allowing for the proper exploitation of the options available to the poet, we can adjust the raw numbers derived from the text to a presumed standard or pattern adopted by the poet. There are different ways to arrive at a compromise figure, and while it may not be possible to achieve a mechanically perfect symmetry through these calculations, it comes very close without the use of surgery or force, and without violating the rules or usages of the language.[5]

5. In the discussion that follows, we will make an arbitrary choice, but one with a certain rational justification in the light of the discussion above: we will assume that the long form of the second m.s. suffix was used in all instances of our eight key-words, and in bound constructions involving a key-word in the construct state, with the suffix being attached to the adjoining absolute noun. We will regard all other instances of this suffix (whether attached to verbs, nouns, or prepositions) as short. In addition we will regard as long all cases of the second m.s. perfect verb, in accordance with the single example of the fully written form in v. 4 (*ṣwyth*; cf. *ṣwyt*, v. 138). Finally, we will read the conjunction *wĕ* at the beginning of v. 41 as a separate syllable, which it almost certainly was at the time of composition or first utterance. We do not claim that this reconstruction reflects the exact set of conditions at the time of composition. All that we claim is that it is a reasonable representation

Before we turn to the tables, charts, and numbers specifically, we will consider one or two possible changes in the text of MT, modest by most standards, but nonetheless emendations of the received text. We are concerned here only with difficulties in the text as they affect the syllable-counts and, in particular, the presence or absence of the almost ubiquitous second m.s. [[65]] pronominal suffix. Three cases were mentioned earlier and the textual evidence cited. We now review them briefly:

(1) Three words in v. 48 almost precisely duplicate three words in v. 47. Many scholars regard this as a good example of vertical dittography, especially as we have good evidence (from the Qumran Psalms Scroll) that the poem was written stichometrically at an early stage in its transmission.

(47) . . . *bĕmiṣwōtêkā ʾăšer ʾāhābtî*
(48) . . . *ʾel-miṣwōtêkā ʾăšer ʾāhābtî*

The three repeated words in v. 48 make it excessively long. They hardly correspond to the context of the verse, whereas they fit quite properly in v. 47. If each verse began with a new line, as shown in the printed versions (or the Psalms Scroll), then the possibility of error would be increased, e.g.,

(47) ואשתעשע במצותיך אשר אהבתי
(48) ואשא כפי אל מצותיך אשר אהבתי

There is unfortunately no textual or versional evidence to support the deletion of the three duplicated words in v. 48, which means that the error, if it is one, occurred very early in the transmission of the text. Much hinges on this point, because the first duplicated word, *miṣwōtêkā*, is one of the eight key-words in the poem. The exact counting and arrangement of these words in relation to each other (they occur in pairs, each having a mate) and to the whole complex structure of the poem, depend to some extent on whether the word here, *mṣwtyk*, is part of the original poem or not. As already noted in the first part of this study (Freedman, [1995]), without this second *mṣwtyk* (v. 48, accidentally copied from v. 47), the total for the eight key-words of the poem as a whole would be 176, the expected symmetrical number (i.e., one key-word per line in the 176-line poem). This perfect symmetry is disturbed by its presence in v. 48. But the case is not that simple, for there are other candidates for dittography, one or two of which make as good sense as this one. Furthermore, the poem is not only not precisely symmetrical in other respects (e.g., the eight key-words do not each occur 22 times, which might be expected in a symmetrical structure), but there seems to be a pattern of distortion, reflected in a series of deviations from the established norms throughout the

---

of the original poem with a vocalization and syllable-count consistent with what we know of the language and its transmission in the biblical period and the early post-biblical era, reflecting also a plausible interpretation of the "16-syllable" tradition recorded by Eusebius.

poem. In view of the numerous instances in which the poet deliberately distorts and deviates from an otherwise symmetrical structure, in which key-words are doubled up or omitted in the different stanzas (and it [[66]] would take an almost unlimited amount of emending and restructuring to cure all of these deviations), it becomes more reasonable to suppose that this poet has adopted an asymmetrical pattern, and spread the ensuing distortions throughout the subdivisions of the poem. Therefore, while it is likely that some dittography has occurred, I would be inclined to limit it to the two-word clause, *ʾăšer ʾāhabtî*, which should be excluded from v. 48 as a scribal error, and retain *miṣwōtêkā* in the same line, even if the resulting sentence makes very awkward Hebrew, and any attempt at adequate translation remains extremely difficult. "And I will raise my palms to your commandments . . ." hardly commends itself. Simply reading *ʾēlêkā* for *ʾel-miṣwōtêkā* would make better sense: "And I will raise my palms to you" (cf. Lam 3:41, where the same idiom is used and the object of raising the palms is *ʾēl baššāmāyim*). Our conclusion is that while MT is certainly suspect, frequently emended by scholars, it may well reflect the original or at least an earlier stage of text; for statistical purposes and our calculations, we will retain the MT while indicating what difference the alternate reading might make in the numbers, tables, and charts.

(2) In v. 49, MT reads *dābār*, while the Psalms Scroll has *dbrykh* (for *dĕbārêkā*, "your words") and LXX has *ton logon sou* (= *dĕbārĕkā*, "your word"). The latter two texts attest to the presence of the second m.s. suffix (for "Yahweh" as everywhere else in the poem), while MT omits the suffix. It is clear from the context, and the poem generally, that *dābār* here must refer to "the word of Yahweh," as elsewhere in the poem, and that *dābār* is one of the eight key-words in the poem repeated throughout the stanzas. Thus, there can be little doubt about the intent of the author: the meaning or sense does not require the actual presence of the pronominal suffix, and that it is implied from the context is obvious. All in all, it looks as though MT has the more difficult and hence the more original reading, while both LXX and 11QPs[a] represent expansions designed to spell out the meaning of the term more exactly. LXX retains the singular noun, but adds the suffix, while 11QPs[a] makes the noun plural in addition to adding the suffix. The order of priority would seem to be the order of expansion: MT has the basic text, on which both LXX and 11QPs[a] are based, and which each adapted as generally correct interpretations of MT (certainly in the case of the pronominal suffix, less likely in the case of the plural noun). This is the only case of the use of *dābār* without the pronominal suffix in the category of key-words (i.e., those associated with and assigned to Yahweh), and therefore quite exceptional. That does not mean, however, that it is wrong, the result of scribal error. On the contrary, our poet is very much interested in exceptions and creates a [[67]] number of them. The readings in LXX and 11QPs[a] can also be explained in terms of a tendency to make all forms conform to the established pattern.

(3) In v. 128, MT has a reading so difficult that scribal error is the likely cause. A different text is evident in each of the readings found in LXX and 11QPs[a]:

MT: *kol-piqqûdê kōl*
LXX: *kol-piqqûdêkā* (*pasas tas entolas sou*)
11QPs[a]: *piqqûdê kôl* (*pqwdy kwl*)

MT makes little sense with the repetition of *kl* before and after the noun *pqwdy*. The simplest emendation is to follow the evidence of LXX and delete the *lamed* at the end of the second *kl*, reading *kol-piqqûdêkā*. The Psalms Scroll has another reading, grammatically sound, but difficult to understand: "the visitations of all." In this instance, MT looks like a conflation of the two readings in LXX and 11QPs[a], an indication of its secondary and derivative status. LXX seems to reflect the more original reading, while 11QPs[a] has a more difficult and perhaps independent reading.

While we have accepted or recommended changes from MT in two of the three cases cited, we will follow MT when making numerical calculations and when constructing the charts and tables to follow, and only in the discussion or explanation of these charts will we deal with the minor differences that changes in the text would entail. While it is important to establish as precise and accurate and original a text as possible (recognizing that MT has no inherent or a priori claim to such a status), we need to avoid any indication or even appearance of altering the data in order to fit some scheme or preconceived structure that we claim to find in the poem. The changes we have considered affect directly certain of the key-words basic to the structure of the whole, although many others could also warrant attention. Our purpose is to show that the surviving text in its present form exhibits very strongly the features to which we have called attention.

We now wish to chart the frequency and distribution of second m.s. suffixed forms in the poem, and add the other variable forms to reach the desired adjustment or compromise between maximum and minimum syllable-counts in the Psalm (see table, p. 69). [[68]] We begin with the minimum count and add the instances of *-kā* as spelled out in the table, and then those of *-tā*, and finally the single case of *wĕ* (v. 41), to arrive at the following totals: [[69]]

	Min. Count	*-kā*	*-tā*	*-wĕ*	
I–XI	1308	84	2	1	= 1395
XII–XXII	1331	85	4	0	= 1420
Total	2639	169	6	1	= 2815

If we were to adopt the proposed emendations, the numbers would come out as follows:

Eight Key-Words
(with and without second m.s. suffix)

Stanza	with -*k*	without -*k*	Bound Expression with -*k*	Bound Expression without -*k*	with -*k*	without -*k*	Total
I–XI							
אמרה	8	0	0	0	8	0	8
דבר	10[6]	1	0	0	10	1	11
חקים	14	0	0	0	14	0	14
מצות	12	0	0	0	12	0	12
משפט	6	1	3	0	9	1	10
עדות	8	1	1	0	9	1	10
פקורים	10	0	0	0	10	0	10
תורה	11	0	1	1	12	1	13
Subtotal	79	3	5	1	84	4	88
XII–XXII							
אמרה	10	0	1	0	11	0	11
דבר	11	0	0	0	11	0	11
חקים	8	0	0	0	8	0	8
מצות	9	0	0	1	9	1	10
משפט	8	2	3	0	11	2	13
עדות	13	0	0	0	13	0	13
פקורים	10[7]	0	0	1	10	1	11
תורה	12	0	0	0	12	0	12
Subtotal	81	2	4	2	85	4	89
Total	160	5	9	3	169	8	177

	Min. Count	-*kā*	-*tā*	-*wĕ*	
I–XI	1309	85	2	1	= 1397
XII–XXII	1330	86	4	0	= 1420
Total	2639	171	6	1	= 2817

6. If we adopt the proposed emendation in v. 49 (*dbrk* for *dbr*), then the chart would be 11 0 0 0 11 0 11.

7. If we adopt the proposed emendation in v. 128 (*pqwdyk* for *pqwdy kl*), then the numbers would be 11 0 0 0 11 0 11.

We will provide charts and tables for all three syllable-counting systems: minimum and maximum, and then the calculated compromise described above, or target plan. Comments will be devoted mainly to the last of the three. Reasonable controls are present for the stanzas and lines or verses, as their boundaries are rigidly determined by the alphabetic scheme. As the charts show, the units, whether lines or stanzas, vary widely in length from each other and from the norm or average. The norm for the stanzas is 128 syllables (8 lines × 16 syllables = 128), but as it happens, we have only one stanza (VII in the third column; there are none in the other columns) that comes out exactly at that number (Table A; see p. 82). Nevertheless, there is a general concentration in the range between 125 and 131 (roughly 2.5% variation), with half of the stanzas (11 in all) within this rather narrow range (with the median between 127 and 128). Put another way, the number below 127 (nine) is equal to the number above 128 (nine), leaving four clustered around the midpoint. The remainder are distributed between 112 at the short end and 146 on the high side, with six between 112 and 122, and five between 134 and 146. The distribution is generally symmetrical (like a bell-shaped curve; Table B). What is clear is that there is no way to make the stanzas equal in length or even approximately so without drastic and unjustified surgery. At the same time, the average and median show that the distribution is not haphazard, and that there is a basic recognition of the norm of 16 syllables per line, as well as 128 syllables per stanza. The link between a presumed norm and the widely varying lengths of both lines and stanzas can only be some purposeful and calculated principle and process of compensation: it seems clear that longer stanzas are balanced against shorter ones, with a number in the middle ⟦70⟧ to establish the norm. The same principle is applicable to individual lines as well, and the whole composition reflects the clear and profound intent of the poet.

We can be quite certain in almost all cases where the lines begin and end, because they are marked in every instance by an alphabetic token (as is true of Lamentations 3). Therefore, except in cases of scribal error, one can be confident about the length of the individual lines as well. In a poem of this length, and with such structural features, there is a high probability that most of the lines are intact and come to us as they came from the mouth or hand of the composer. Once again, it is clear that the lines reflect the same patterns already observed in regard to the stanzas: wide variation in the length of individual lines, but clustering symmetrically around the norm and median (16 syllables for the bicolon or line), with the principle of compensation applied to produce a symmetrical structure. The approach, method, and procedure are very similar to what we have already observed with respect to the eight key-words: a simple structural scheme in which individual items are arranged in a variety of ways with subtle modifications, comparable to musical compositions consisting of a simple theme and then a series of increasingly subtle and complicated variations, both concealing and revealing the original theme and the endless possibilities in developing and expanding it, ultimately revealing a very complex and sophisticated mind at work.

The chart of line-length and distribution shows the following (Table C): Of the 176 lines, 34 have exactly sixteen syllables, while an additional 70 are within one syllable of sixteen (39 have 15 and 31 have 17). Thus we have a total of 104 lines within a range of one syllable of the norm, and that represents nearly 60% of the total. If we extend our range to two syllables from the norm, we add another 38 lines (16 have 14 syllables, while 22 have 18 syllables), making a total of 142 lines out of 176, or well over 80% of the total. If one assumes the cluster in the range of 15 to 17 syllables as the median, then there are the same number of lines below fifteen and above seventeen (36 lines in the range from 12 to 14, and 36 lines in the range from 18 to 23). The wide range from 12 to 23 syllables (we may suspect that the lines over twenty syllables may have been expanded unintentionally and some scribal errors may be involved, as already noted) shows that although the poet felt free to wander far afield from his norm in composing individual lines, he nevertheless was able to integrate everything into the prevailing pattern. It is possible that some of the shorter lines are defective and some of the longer lines are overloaded, but the phenomenon at both extremes is far too extensive to be regarded as a kind of double contamination. The principle of [[71]] compensation, on the other hand, will account for both longer and shorter lines quite adequately, and in fact it is precisely the presence of both that points away from accidental error to deliberate planning. Since the same phenomenon in different guises turns up repeatedly in this poem, there is every reason to believe that the same principle and method are at work when it comes to metrical considerations.

When it comes to individual cola or half-lines, we do not have the same rigorous guideposts or markers provided by the letters of the alphabet for the lines (bicola) and stanzas, and certainty in determining where the pause or division occurs in each line can hardly be achieved in all cases. In most instances, however, the presence of the *athnach* (pause) and the grammatical and syntactic structure of the lines make the division highly likely. In the remaining examples, and especially where the *athnach* is not present, we have made what seems to be the most reasonable division (acknowledging in some instances more than one possible division and, in a few cases, no clear division at all). We might infer that run-on lines do exist in Hebrew poetry, and that therefore a metrical division might not conform to a grammatical or syntactic division, as commonly in English poetry. Normally, however, as is clearly the case with full lines, there is a noticeable grammatical break at the end of the metrical unit. Allowing for some slight uncertainty about where half-lines or cola begin and end, one can draw reasonable conclusions from the far greater number in which there is little or no doubt. The principle conclusion is the same as that found for bicola and stanzas: there is a wide range of variation in length for half-lines or cola, accompanied by a pronounced clustering around a center-point with a symmetrical balancing of longer and shorter units by compensation.

The apparent norm in this balanced-line poem is eight syllables per colon, one-half of the sixteen-syllable bicolon or verse (as described by Eusebius). Of the 352 cola in the poem, 99 have eight syllables and comprise the largest single group in the entire work, far more verses than for any other single-line length (Table D). In view of the many factors noted above affecting line-length and syllable-counting, if one adds to the central cluster those cola of seven and nine syllables each, there are 68 with seven syllables (per colon) and 66 with nine syllable for a subtotal of 134, resulting in a sum of 233 out of a total of 352, or 66.2% for all those within one syllable of the norm. In other words, almost two-thirds of the total number of half-lines or cola come within one syllable of the norm, reflecting considerable regularity amid all the variety and deviation in individual cases. If one further adds a two-syllable difference at the low and high ends, there are 43 cola of six syllables and 35 [[72]] of ten syllables. These 78 added to the 233 already accounted for result in a total of 311 or 88.4% of 352. While most of the cola are within what might be called a standard range of variation in metrical poetry, a sizable number are not included, enough to show that very notable deviations from the established pattern were regarded as permissible and belonged to the creative options of the poet. We have cola as short as four syllables and as long as 14 or 15 syllables. This variety raises the question whether grammatical divisions always reflect the metrical intentions of the poet, or whether such lines should be divided in consideration of metrical rather than grammatical or syntactic factors. There is also the question whether in half-lines of such extreme length (14 and 15 syllables) there may be an additional colon in the verse (not uncommon in Hebrew poetry), or whether such lines contain scribal errors (especially dittography). There is often a tension between syntax and meter in poetry generally, and reconciling different analyses may be more a matter of deciding how to place the words on the page, i.e., the appearance of the lines in relation to each other, than any difficulty in the poetry itself.

A provisional judgment is that the poet had certain metrical principles and goals in mind, and these can be defined in terms of the overall length of the work and the average length of the line, along with a clustering or concentration of lines of the same length to form the bulk of the lines in the poem. Along with this central cluster, there will be moderate and even drastic deviations in terms of line length, both longer and shorter, but by and large these will balance off against each other to produce the originally intended and inescapable effect of symmetry. The pattern is the same at all levels (cola, lines, stanzas): clustering around the norm with moderate to extreme deviation at the periphery. No serious effort seems to have been made to achieve strict metrical uniformity at any of these levels; on the contrary, deliberate deviation from an established norm seems to be the norm. The same pattern is repeated: clustering or concentration around the norm, with wide but deliberate deviations, controlled by the pervasive principle of compensation to achieve the goal of balance or symmetry in the overall arrangement. This schema is found repeatedly in Hebrew poetry, and is by no means restricted to artificial alphabetic acrostic poems such as this one, or to late didactic poetry, or to any class or age of poem in the Biele.

We now attempt to interpret Eusebius' statement about the Great Psalm's composition in hexameter as some sort of accentual or stress system in the Hebrew poem. It is extremely difficult, if not impossible, to deduce from or impose upon Hebrew poetry any sort of regular quantitative metrical structure characteristic of Greek and Latin poetry (i.e., with repeated feet containing the [[73]] same sequence of stressed and unstressed, long and short syllables). One can nevertheless speak loosely of a quantitative meter in which lines contain roughly the same number of syllables divided between stressed and unstressed. In this way, we interpret Eusebius to mean that the basic pattern of Psalm 119 contains lines of sixteen syllables, six syllables of which are accented or stressed, with the caesura normally dividing such lines in the middle into half-lines or cola of eight syllables and three accents each.

Having studied the syllable counts, we can now turn to the stress patterns in the poem. To carry out this investigation, we will follow MT as closely as possible, identifying all the accents and including those marked with *metheg*, which at least implies a secondary stress. As is generally known, MT reflects wide variations in the use of accents (the system was intended for chanting and to indicate intonation, but our interest is confined to distinguishing between stressed and unstressed syllables) and a certain lack of consistency. In different contexts, the same word (especially one-syllable particles) may or may not receive an accent, or they may be connected to the next word by a *maqqep* and lose the accent or receive a *metheg* in its place. Generally, content words (nouns and verbs) are accented, but not always, especially when two words are linked by *makkeph*. All in all, Masoretes exercised considerable freedom in marking accents, no doubt reflecting both the actual practice in chanting the Scriptures in their own day along with a long-standing tradition. It is not difficult to argue that in some cases the accentuation in MT seems arbitrary, and runs contrary to normal practice or even good sense. Overall, however, MT is quite regular and rational, and the differences between what is recorded in MT and what might be regarded as a rational, neutral approach are relatively minor and do not affect general impressions and major tendencies.

The major surprise is that the accentual count, whatever system is used, hardly confirms the statement in Eusebius. Although the syllable counts conform to the tradition recorded by Eusebius, the number and distribution of accents or stresses suggest something at variance with the "hexameters" announced by the Church Father. In this connection we note first of all a marked tendency for the first colon in each line to outweigh or be longer than the second one. Thus, while eight-syllable cola seem to be evenly distributed between A and B positions, longer cola are concentrated in the first position, and shorter cola in the second position. The overall picture can be summarized in the following fashion: [[74]]

	A (colon)	B (colon)		Total
Stanzas 1–11	737 +	658	=	1395
Stanzas 12–22	742 +	678	=	1420
Total	1479 +	1336	=	2815

Those are the figures for the target plan or compromise solution. The numbers derived from the short and long counts are comparable.

	Short Count					Long Count				
	A		B		Total	A		B		Total
Stanzas 1–11	777	+	601	=	1308	762	+	682	=	1444
Stanzas 12–22	710	+	621	=	1331	769	+	689	=	1458
Total	1417	+	1222	=	2639	1531	+	1371	=	2902

The pattern is the same in both major parts of the poem: the A cola consistently outweigh the B cola, as the numbers show. There is a variation of one syllable per colon throughout the poem. While the difference is not great, it is sufficient to show that it is deliberate. Within the larger numerical symmetry, there is a patterned deviation that lays greater weight on the first colon throughout the poem, confirmed by the number and distribution of the accents. The accompanying tables show that the first cola are more heavily accented than the second cola in the poem, whether one includes the instances of *metheg* in the count or not. If the hexameter pattern were actually applied, one would expect 528 accents in the A cola and 528 in the B cola. The actual range for the A cola is from 509 accents to 538 (including the cases of *metheg*), whose range encompasses the desired total and reflects the three-accents-per-colon meter. For the B cola, however, the range extends from 437 (accents) to 449 (with *metheg*), which is substantially below the expected number of 528. Many of the bicola have a pattern of 3 + 2 = 5 accents rather than 3 + 3 = 6, but the overall schema does not conform to a 3 + 2 = 5 pattern, since that would produce a total of 528 + 352 = 880, considerably lower than our total. The numbers for the B cola actually straddle the intermediate number half-way between 3 accents and 2 accents for the second colon: 440 (we count 437 accents and 449 if we add the occurrences of *metheg*). In other words, within the standard sixteen-syllable [[75]] line, we have a slight imbalance between the A-cola and the B-cola, which is nevertheless reflected not only in the internal syllable counts, but even more markedly in the number and distribution of the accents. The meter is clearly not 3:3 or 3:2, but a mixture of the two, in effect an equal number of lines or bicola that are 3:3 and 3:2. The effect is present, but not as pronounced as it would be if both syllables and accents conformed to one pattern or the other,[8] but a mixture that, while preserving a balanced syllable count, gives the impression of a slightly falling rhythm.

In the poem overall, there is a preponderance of accents in the first colon, and that is true also of the syllable counts (Table A). The difference is that the total number of syllables corresponds to the expected norm, whereas the accent count remains unbalanced and does not. What all this means for the present investigation is that syllable counts are more reliable and more indicative of the underlying structure of a poem than accent counts. In other words, all syllables were regarded as of approximately equal value without regard to accent, and an eight-syllable colon with two accents was considered equivalent to an eight-syllable colon with three accents (i.e., that discrepancy was either ignored or an accent was arbitrarily added to the colon with only two natural accents). Often, as in this poem, MT simply does not provide the expected third accent. The effect is to weight the cola in favor of the first unit rather than the second. Our poet does not go as far in this direction as the poet of Lamentations 1–3, where line-length is modified in the direction of the 3:2 pattern of accents by the 8:5 (some 7:6) syllable counts. In Psalm 119 the largest single group happens to have the 3:2 accent count: 64 (Table E, Proposed Count). The expected standard 3:3 rhythm occurs only in 54 bicola, while the count for other balanced bicola is 2:2 = 4 and 4:4 = 1. Unbalanced lines go both ways. Those with the added weight or length on the first colon are the dominant group with 95 occurrences (4:2 = 14; 4:3 = 13; 5:2 = 1; 5:3 = 2; 5:4 = 1; 6:2 = 1; 6:3 = 1; 3:2 = 62). Those unbalanced in the opposite direction number 22 (2:3 = 13; 2:4 = 3; 3:4 = 6).

As expected, the three-beat colon is dominant in this poem. The surprise is the number of cola with only two beats, almost half as many as the three-

8. This appears in Lamentations 1–3, where the meter is predominantly 3:2 and the syllable count is 13 overall (representing 8 + 5 = 13 and 7 + 6 = 13).

beat cola. Four-beat cola are much less frequent, and five-beat cola are very rare. The dominant three-beat cola are fairly well balanced with a modest but significant majority in the first colon (122:83; Table E, Proposed Count). With respect to two-beat cola, the ratio is heavily weighted in the [[76]] opposite direction (20:82). The four-beat and five-beat cola are predominantly in the first position as expected (four-beat [28:11] and five-beat [4:0]). The data can be summarized in the following table:

	COLA		ACCENTS	
	A	B	A	B
(2)	20	82	40	164
(3)	122	83	366	249
(4)	28	11	112	44
(5)	4	0	20	0
(6)	2	0	12	0
TOTAL	176	176	550	457

In the A-colon the dominant number is three beats, and the higher counts more than balance the lower ones: the norm would be 528, and the evidence shows 550, slightly more than expected. In the B-colon, we would expect the same number (528) in a balanced meter or rhythm, but the actual count is considerably below that figure: 457. The B-cola are almost equally divided between two-beat and three-beat units, with a very slight preference for the latter, reinforced by a handful of four-beat cola. What is unusual is the large number of two-beat cola in a poem with an essentially balanced rhythmic structure, the hypothetical norm for which is a syllable count of 8 + 8 = 16 and an accentual count of 3 + 3 = 6. The divergence or modification is too pronounced to be regarded as the result of inadvertence or happenstance. At the same time, the poet has not adopted the falling rhythm (the so-called *qinah*-meter, or 3:2) so characteristic of the book of Lamentations (chaps. 1–4). Instead, he has tipped the balance metrically (syllables regardless of accent) in favor of the first colon as opposed to the second, so that there is a clear impression of first-colon preference, but it is just as clearly within the framework of the standard balanced meter that is typical of the greater part of Hebrew poetry. The poet has taken advantage of the principle of equivalence, whereby cola with the same number of syllables may well differ in respect to the number of accents but still be regarded as metrically equal. While there are a number of exceptions, the charts show that there is a preponderance of accents and syllables in the A-colon compared with the B-colon. The only constant is the total number of syllables (for the poem), whose total is as [[77]] anticipated, although the range between minimal and maximal counts is so great (about 10%) that fixing the number is somewhat arbitrary. At least it can be said that the projected number (176 lines × 16 syllables = 2,816 syllables; our resultant number is 2,815) falls between the extremes, and might well be regarded as the poet's target, if not the standard, in composing this piece. Put another way, one might say that given the poet's clear intention to modify the standard, evenly-balanced, metrical structure in this poem, he felt that it was obligatory to meet the syllable-counting requirement overall, while not regarding the accentual norm as binding. As a result, the total number of accents or beats in the poem is (A) 550 + (B) 457 = 1007 (an approximation, including most accents and *methegs* in MT), which is substantially lower than the expected total of (A) 528 + (B) 528 = 1056. It is possible that the difference (about 5%) was not regarded as significant, although given the greater precision in most other matters, including syllable-counting, I would doubt that the difference in accent-counting was negligible. Or it may be that the poet used accents on words and syllables that are not indicated in MT, and so imagined that the presumed accent requirement was fulfilled. My own impression is that the accentual norm was not regarded as firm or binding, and that poets, like the Masoretes, allowed themselves considerable leeway in placing or not placing accents on the same words and syllables, contingent upon context, euphony, or other criteria. While it is convenient and helpful to identify different rhythmic and metrical structures by a supposed accentual system (3:3, or 3:2, or 2:2, or the like), a system adopted traditionally and almost universally by scholars as though it actually were the system used by the poets of the Hebrew Bible, the fact remains that it is not very accurate or precise, that MT reflects wide disparities in the use of accents (and *methegs*), and that the resulting numbers do not balance out very well. It should be recognized as a very imperfect way of describing the poetic phenomena under consideration. Counting all syllables and not just accented ones gives a better picture of the principles and procedures employed in biblical Hebrew poetry, and attests more reliably to the interest in and concern for symmetrical structures on the part of the Hebrew poet.

Summary

We may now summarize the findings of the investigation of Psalm 119. The poem is structured in a highly intricate way, beginning with the alphabetic acrostic pattern: each of the 22 stanzas corresponding to the 22 letters of the Hebrew alphabet has eight lines, each of which begins with the same letter appropriate to that stanza. This structure is linked emphatically to the central [[78]] theme of the poem: the celebration of 'the Law of the Lord' (תורת יהוה,

v. 1). In keeping with the eight-line stanza,[9] the poet has chosen eight key-words, beginning with *torah* (*primus inter pares* as shown by the varying frequencies) and supplemented by seven others, all roughly synonymous or sharing an extended semantic field. These eight words are then repeated systematically throughout the poem, on an average of one per line, 22 times per word, for a total approximating the total number of lines in the poem (176). The actual total is 177, a discrepancy of one from the ideal and expected number. The difference may be due to scribal error in transmission, or it may represent a deliberate distortion of a presumed perfect number. There is enough evidence of deliberate departure from or modification of the ideal numbers to make firm judgments in this area precarious, and it may well be that along with the simple, symmetrical, and perfect underlying pattern, there is an equally deliberate and intentional pattern of variation and even distortion. Nevertheless, in keeping with the persistent pattern of bilateral symmetry, four of the eight words are feminine and four are masculine. While the evidence is less decisive, there may also have been an equal division between singular and plural (in the surviving manuscripts of MT, there is some confusion between singular and plural forms, especially in the case of the words *dābār* and *mišpāṭ*). Thus, one expects and does find the eight words divided by pairs into fem. sing. and plural, and masc. sing. and plural. As we observed in comparing the actual numbers (which vary from a low of 19 to a high of 25 in frequency), the two words sharing number and gender form a pair, and the total number of the two in every case is 44 (e.g., אמרה [f.s. 19] + תורה [f.s. 25] = 44, but the case with the masculine nouns is different). Throughout, there are other minor variations in usage, showing that the poet was not the slave but the master of the system.

Most, but not all, of the lines of the poem have one and only one of these key words (as observed above, four of the lines of the poem do not have any of the key words, while four or five have two of them). We deplore the persistent efforts of scholars to improve upon the original by emending the text to supply the missing words in the four lines that do not have them, and to force perfection (or monotony) on the poem in spite of the clear indications that the poet did not wish to achieve that kind of precision, or transcended [[79]] simple symmetry by invoking higher laws of aesthetic variation and complexity. In fact only 167 (or possibly 168) lines correspond to the rule or expectation, enough to show what the underlying principle was, but not enough to rule out deliberate deviation from that norm in the case of eight (!)

9. The selection of the number eight may result from the notion that the eight acts of creation in Genesis 1 reflect the perfection of the universe as crated by God, and the resulting correspondence between the law as the perfect expression and the universe as the perfect creation of the same God.

or nine lines. As noted, four of the lines (vv. 3, 37, 90 and 122) do not have any of the key-words, while four or five of them (vv. 16, 48, 160, 168 and 172) have two key-words each, thereby reaching or exceeding the desired total. What is manifest here is the fundamental and pervasive principle of compensation, whereby a deficiency in one place is made up for in another place by an addition. When it comes to the distribution of key-words in the stanzas, we find an even greater diversity in the actual placement of the different words. To begin with, not one of the key-words occurs in every stanza; at the same time, some occur twice in some stanzas to make up for their omission in others. One (תורה) even occurs three times in one stanza (in this way exploiting some of the surplus that it enjoys in the pairing with אמרה, which occurs fewer times and is lacking in several stanzas). The stanzas themselves vary in the number of key-words they contain. While the largest single group has the expected eight (one per line), the actual distribution of a different one in each of the eight lines is relatively rare; several have only seven, while the remainder have nine, again illustrating the principle of compensation. Surprisingly, only five of the stanzas have each of the eight words only once, the optimum and ideal arrangement, while all of the others have omissions and/or duplications. Even among the few that have the eight different key-words once each, there is a difference in the order and arrangement. The result is that although the basic structure is simple and repeatable, no two stanzas are identical in selection, number, arrangement, and order. If they agree in one or two respects, they will differ in at least one of the others. So in the larger picture they are the same, but they vary in detail. The variety is unending, but always carefully contained in and constrained by the overall symmetrical pattern. Undoubtedly there are many other mechanical and technical features in the poem, such as the selection and distribution of other nouns and verbs, which deserve to be studied for evidence of symmetrical planning and deliberate deviation. We will leave those for future study at another time and no doubt for other scholars to pursue.

When it comes to metrical analysis and considerations, we believe that the same basic principles hold: that there is an underlying or overriding pattern, and with it considerable deliberate variation and deviation controlled by target numbers, the goal of symmetry, and the principle of compensation. We began with the statement of the Church Father Eusebius, Bishop of Caesarea, that ⟦80⟧ this poem along with the Song of Moses (Deuteronomy 32), which we hope to discuss in another place, consists of hexameters of sixteen syllables. On the basis of careful counting and checking, we have determined that the statement should be taken seriously, may be based on authentic tradition if not direct knowledge on the part of Eusebius, and can be defended as objectively true if understood in a specific way. The rule cannot be applied rigorously to each line of the poem, although in fact many of the lines actually have sixteen syllables, and many more are only a syllable away from that number. There remain too many others that deviate significantly from that key-number for it to be the rule for every line of the poem. Nevertheless, these deviations themselves are not random or haphazard, but form a pattern of their own. To explain this we invoke two principles, which are themselves interlocking and overlapping: (1) if we understand the statement to mean that the *average* line length is sixteen syllables, then by adding up all of the syllables in the lines and dividing by their number, we find that the most reasonable conclusion conforms to the ancient statement; and (2) correspondingly, there seems to be a deliberate effort to match up long lines with short lines, so that they pair off at the mean or average, just as we have already observed regarding the eight key-words. Thus we can identify the principle of balance, and the method of compensation or pairing, to achieve symmetry.

Regarding the "hexameters" mentioned by Eusebius, we interpret the Greek terms as referring to or reflecting the accentual system in Hebrew. While as in the case of the overall syllable counts there are many lines with six accents (often dividing in the middle, i.e., 3:3), there are many others (too many to accommodate easily) that have fewer accents, and some that have more accents. In the case of accents, we cannot invoke the principles and procedures we used in counting all the syllables, and therefore cannot conclude that the divergences from the presumed norm balance out, or that lines with more accents compensate for lines with fewer accents. In short, we cannot confirm the statement by Eusebius. On the contrary, we have to state that according to our present knowledge, too many lines do not conform to the stated pattern, and we cannot invoke the principles of symmetry and compensation to account for the divergence from the presumed norm. Overall, there is a notable preponderance of accents in the first colon of bicola in the poem, and often a lower number in the second colon, so that alongside the expected 3:3 pattern, there are almost as many lines with a 3:2 pattern. The remaining lines vary in a different fashion, and clearly do not suffice to correct the apparent imbalance created by the numerous 3:2 lines in the poem. This overbalance or extra weight on the first colon in contrast with the second [[81]] colon is also reflected in the overall syllable count, confirming the shift away from the presumed norm. In the latter case, we were able to invoke the principles and procedures of balance and compensation to reflect the sixteen-syllable norm. That is not the case with the accentual patterns.

In sum, the poem is a mechanical and technical marvel, with an intricately worked structure, within which the poet exercised considerable freedom to express his originality and creativity, while keeping within the self-imposed boundaries of the overall construction.[10]

10. This paper was prepared with the assistance of Andrew J. Welch.

Bibliography

Briggs, C. A., and Briggs, E. G. 1909. *Psalms.* International Critical Commentary, Volume 2. New York.

Freedman, D. N. 1980. "Acrostics and Metrics in Hebrew Poetry." *Pottery, Poetry, and Prophecy,* 51–76. Winona Lake.

_______ . [1995]. "The Structure of Psalm 119: Part I." [[*Pomegranates and Golden Bells: Studies in Ritual, Law, and Literature in Honor of Jacob Milgrom* (ed. David P. Wright, David Noel Freedman, and Avi Hurvitz; Winona Lake, Ind.: Eisenbrauns) 725–56]]. Reprinted here as chapter 2.

Gray, G. B. 1972. *The Forms of Hebrew Poetry.* New York.

Kraus, H. J. 1989. *Psalms 60–150: A Commentary.* Minneapolis.

Levenson, J. D. 1987. "The Sources of Torah: Psalm 119 and the Modes of Revelation in Second Temple Judaism." *Ancient Israelite Religion,* pp. 559–74. Eds. P. D. Miller, Jr., P. D. Hanson, and S. D. McBride. Philadelphia.

Sanders, J. A. 1967. *The Dead Sea Psalms Scroll.* Ithaca.

Soll, W. 1991. *Psalm 119: Matrix, Form and Setting.* Catholic Biblical Quarterly Monograph Series 23. Washington.

TABLE A
SYLLABLES BY STANZA

	Low Count			High Count			Proposed		
Stanza	A	B	Total	A	B	Total	A	B	Total
I	52	55	107	55	61	116	54	58	112
II	58	48	106	64	57	121	62	53	115
III	60	56	116	63	64	127	62	63	125
IV	61	53	114	64	61	125	64	58	122
V	70	48	118	78	53	131	76	49	125
VI	82	51	133	89	58	147	87	56	143
VII	67	54	121	71	59	130	69	59	128
VIII	68	54	122	72	64	136	68	62	130
IX	52	59	111	55	67	122	54	66	120
X	78	60	138	85	68	153	80	66	146
XI	59	63	122	66	70	136	61	68	129
Subtotal	707	601	1308	762	682	1444	737	658	1395
XII	65	54	119	70	60	130	68	59	127
XIII	68	54	122	73	57	130	73	57	130
XIV	62	57	119	66	65	131	65	62	127
XV	65	60	125	70	66	136	69	65	134
XVI	61	54	115	69	58	127	62	58	120
XVII	59	60	119	64	65	129	62	64	126
XVIII	57	53	110	62	59	121	61	58	119
XIX	65	54	119	68	62	130	66	61	127
XX	68	63	131	71	71	142	70	70	140
XXI	68	53	121	76	58	134	73	57	130
XXII	72	59	131	80	68	148	73	67	140
Subtotal	710	621	1331	769	689	1458	742	678	1420
TOTAL	1417	1222	2639	1531	1371	2902	1479	1336	2815

Averages	Low Count	High Count	Proposed
Bicolon	15.00	16.25	16.00
Colon	7.50	8.25	8.00
Stanza	120.00	132.00	128.00

TABLE B
SYLLABLE COUNT BY STANZAS

Low Count	High Count	Proposed Count
106	116	112
107	121 (2 stanzas)	115
110	122	119
111	125	120 (2 stanzas)
114	127 (2 stanzas)	122
115	129	125 (2 stanzas)
116		126
118	130 (4 stanzas)*	
	131 (2 stanzas)*	127 (3 stanzas)
119 (3 stanzas)*		128 *
121 (2 stanzas)*	134	
	136 (3 stanzas)	129
122 (3 stanzas)	142	130 (3 stanzas)
125	147	134
131 (2 stanzas)	148	140 (2 stanzas)
133	153	143
138		146

* = Median Range

Table C
LINE LENGTHS BY SYLLABLES

	Stanzas 1–11			Stanzas 12–22			Total		
Syllables	Low	High	Prop.	Low	High	Prop.	Low	High	Prop.
11	5	0	0	1	0	0	6	0	0
12	9	3	4	4	1	1	13	4	5
13	9	7	11	9	1	4	18	8	15
14	18	9	9	19	7	7	37	16	16
15	17	15	18	16	16	21	33	31	39
16	10	13	17	22	18	17	32	31	34
17	12	18	9	13	21	22	25	39	31
18	2	5	11	1	13	11	3	18	22
19	3	9	3	2	6	2	5	15	5
20	0	4	3	1	3	2	1	7	5
21	2	2	0	0	2	1	2	4	1
22	1	1	1	0	0	0	1	1	1
23	0	1	2	0	0	0	0	1	2
24	0	1	0	0	0	0	0	1	0

Table D
COLA LENGTH BY SYLLABLES

	Stanzas 1–11			Stanzas 12–22			Total		
Syllables	Low	High	Prop.	Low	High	Prop.	Low	High	Prop.
4	6	4	5	2	1	1	8	5	6
5	15	9	9	4	4	4	19	13	13
6	32	13	24	35	13	19	67	26	43
7	46	33	32	46	33	36	92	66	68
8	37	51	48	48	50	51	85	101	99
9	18	26	26	27	42	40	45	68	66
10	13	19	19	9	20	16	22	39	35
11	6	14	8	4	10	7	10	24	15
12	0	4	2	1	2	1	1	6	3
13	2	1	1	0	1	1	2	2	2
14	1	1	1	0	0	0	1	1	1
15	0	1	1	0	0	0	0	1	1

COLA SYLLABLES BY A AND B COLA

	Low		High		Proposed	
Syllables	A	B	A	B	A	B
4	1	7	1	4	1	5
5	4	15	2	11	2	11
6	24	43	13	13	20	23
7	37	55	23	43	28	40
8	51	34	53	48	50	49
9	30	15	32	36	32	34
10	16	6	23	16	25	10
11	9	1	20	4	12	3
12	1	0	5	1	2	1
13	2	0	2	0	2	0
14	1	0	1	0	1	0
15	0	0	1	0	1	0

TABLE E
BI-COLA BY ACCENTS

Masoretic Text

Accents A+B	Stanzas 1–11	Stanzas 12–22	TOTAL
2+2	13	6	19
2+3	11	15	26
2+4	1	2	3
3+2	32	32	64
3+3	14	22	36
3+4	0	1	1
4+2	8	6	14
4+3	7	3	10
4+4	1	0	1
5+3	1	0	1
5+4	0	1	1

With *Metheg*

Accents A+B	Stanzas 1–11	Stanzas 12–22	TOTAL
2+2	9	5	14
2+3	7	9	16
2+4	0	3	3
3+2	29	29	58
3+3	15	28	43
3+4	2	3	5
4+2	11	5	16
4+3	10	5	15
4+4	1	0	1
5+3	3	0	3
5+4	0	1	1
6+2	1	0	1

Proposed Count

Accents A+B	Stanzas 1–11	Stanzas 12–22	TOTAL
2+2	2	2	4
2+3	7	6	13
2+4	1	2	3
3+2	33	29	62
3+3	22	32	54
3+4	2	4	6
4+2	8	6	14
4+3	7	6	13
4+4	1	0	1
5+2	1	0	1
5+3	2	0	2
5+4	0	1	1
6+2	1	0	1
6+3	1	0	1

Chapter 4

Conclusion: The Theology of Psalm 119

DAVID NOEL FREEDMAN
AND
ANDREW WELCH

Form ever follows function.
—Louis Henry Sullivan

The Reputation of Psalm 119

The preceding two chapters treat Psalm 119, the longest and most complex biblical poem. While scholars have praised the psalm's thoroughness, they have also denigrated its artificial structure, lack of originality, and repetition. Oesterley's (1955: 486) verdict is typical:

> It is largely due to this artificial construction that the composition abounds in repetitions which makes the reading of it somewhat monotonous.

These objections manifest themselves above all in egregious emendation to "correct" the psalm. Since there is a synonym for *tôrâ* in virtually every verse, the argument goes, then the absence of a synonym, or the appearance of two, in a verse must be a sign of textual corruption or authorial sloppiness. Charles Augustus Briggs (1909: 415–16), for example, proposes more than three dozen emendations. Mitchell Dahood (1970), from a very different starting point, suggests even more, though he emends only the vowel pointings. The research presented here should put to rest such attempts to improve Psalm 119.

A dismissive evaluation of the psalm's creativity must also be radically revised. Psalm 119 is, in fact, endlessly inventive—but not according to contemporary standards. In this century, biblical poetry tends to be valued for its powerful images, provocative turns of phrase, or powerful emotional statements (Alter 1985: 111–12; Buttenwieser 1969: 871). (Psalm 137, for instance, captures the essence of exile in three short verses.) The creativity of

Psalm 119 is the creativity of the puzzle-builder, the craftsperson, mathematically rather than metaphorically complex. Such literature may not be to modern taste, but shifting critical criteria cannot efface the psalmist's achievement.

Psalm 119's construction is unique in ancient Near Eastern literature. Will Soll (1991: 6–11), in a survey of non-Israelite acrostic poems, shows that there exist some Mesopotamian parallels but nothing to match the eight alphabetic acrostic psalms of the Hebrew Bible. There are seven extant Babylonian examples, six of which are stanzaic, like Psalm 119. The acrostic syllables produce not an alphabet (impossible, since cuneiform is not alphabetic) but sentences, which reinforce the poem's content and/or identify the poem's author.

The most instructive parallel between the Babylonian and Israelite acrostics is the implicit approval given to the poets' manipulation of language and form: sacred literature is a legitimate arena for authorial wordplay. Moreover, such wordplay can augment the theological message of the poem. The artificiality of Psalm 119, then, can be seen, not as a stultifying structure that kills the poet's creativity, but as the broadest canvass possible for the poet's skill in making the psalm's form assist its function, the praise of *tôrat yhwh.*

While we are on the subject of non-Israelite parallels, it is worth noting that the psalm's repetitive character—which strikes so many commentators as monotonous—has a long, honorable history in ancient Near Eastern poetry, dating back to the earliest Sumerian hymns. Repetitive parallelism is, consequently, commonly taken as a sign of antiquity in Israelite poetry. Psalm 119 is manifestly not an early psalm. But the psalmist's use of repetition can certainly not be ascribed simply to an absence of inspiration or failure of imagination. The psalmist deliberately and intricately employs repetition as part of the poem's grand scheme.

Previous studies also show conclusively that the psalmist is working with 8 key words, not 10. Several commentators, mostly devotional writers of the eighteenth and nineteenth centuries, have argued that there must be 10 key words (adding *derek* and *ʾōraḥ*) in order to create a strict parallel with the Decalogue, the presumed essence of the *tôrat yhwh.* The precise numbers obtained utilizing 8 key words, combined with the 8-line stanzas, show that the poem does not rest on a foundation of 10 key words.

The Apotheosis of tôrâ

The *ʾalep*-to-*taw* structure of Psalm 119 shares with the other acrostic psalms a clear message of totality and completeness—as we would say, "from A to Z." In this psalm, Yahweh's *tôrâ* is the psalmist's joy and delight (vv. 14, 16, 24, 47, 70, 77, 92, 143, 162, and 174), light (v. 105), wealth (vv. 72, 162), and life itself (vv. 25, 50): *tôrat yhwh* is everything to the psalmist, and acrostic form provides apposite reinforcement of the psalmist's message. The acrostic form also expresses the perfection of *tôrat yhwh*: it is wholly divine (v. 89) and wonderful (v. 129). Nothing is missing; no part of *tôrâ* is incomplete. The celebration of the fullness of Yahweh's revelation is implied in the other acrostic psalms (see chap. 1) and, indeed, in the structure of the Hebrew Bible itself. Psalm 119's exhaustiveness sets it apart, from the gross structure of 8-line stanzas to the fine structural details such as the total number of *tôrâ*-words in the psalm: 176 (the number of lines) plus one.

The inexhaustibility of *tôrâ* is the main theme of Psalm 119's structure. Artur Weiser (1962: 740) dismisses the psalm as saying in 176 verses what it takes only v. 1 to say. This is precisely the psalmist's point: a blessed, spotless life (vv. 1, 9) can be found only by immersing oneself in *tôrâ*, by devoting oneself completely to it (vv. 33–35, 54–55). *Tôrâ* has become for the psalmist much more than the laws by which Israel should live, as given in the Pentateuch; *tôrâ* has become a personal way to God. The psalm, then, comes from a time in Israel's history when *tôrâ* is truly a sacred text. As such, it repays infinite study. In fact, *tôrâ* has become the focus of a fixed pattern of prayer seven times daily (v. 164), apparently including midnight (v. 62; the language is identical with v. 164) and the night watches (v. 148).

Despite the primacy of *tôrâ*, however, Psalm 119 never specifies the actual contents of *tôrâ*. The logical assumption is that the psalmist has the Pentateuch in mind. Yet the psalm gives even less information than does Nehemiah 8, the great narrative celebration of *tôrâ* in the Writings, which at least links Moses' name to *tôrâ*. In Psalm 119 *tôrâ* is a monolithic presence, consisting of individual laws and teachings to be sure, but described in only the most general terms, namely the 8 interchangeable *tôrâ*-words. And Psalm 119 omits any human intermediation in the giving of *tôrâ*. *Tôrâ* is Yahweh's alone, primeval (*mēʿôlām*, v. 52) and eternal (*lĕʿôlām*, vv. 89, 144, 152, 160). Moses, Sinai, and covenant all have disappeared.

In short, Psalm 119 gives *tôrâ* virtually the status of a divine hypostasis, like wisdom (*ḥokmâ*) in Proverbs 8. Psalm 119 and Proverbs 8 share vocabulary and theology.[1] Neither *tôrâ* nor *ḥokmâ* can be separated from Yahweh,

1. E.g., *ʾĕmet* 'truth' (Ps 119:43, 142, 151, 160 // Prov 8:7), *ʾōraḥ* 'way' (Ps 119:9, 15, 101, 104, 128 // Prov 8:20), *ʾašrê* 'blessed' (Ps 119:1, 2 // Prov 8:32, 34), *derek* 'way' (Ps 119:1, 3, 5, 14, 26, 27, 29, 30, 32, 33, 37, 59, 168 // Prov 8:2, 13, 22, 32), *kesep* 'silver' (Ps 119:72 // Prov 8:10, 19), *mēʿôlām* 'from eternity' (Ps 119:52 // Prov 8:23), *nātîb* 'path' (Ps 119:35, 105 // Prov 8:2, 20), *paz* 'gold' (Ps 119:127 // Prov 8:19), *pĕtāy/ʾîm* 'fools' (Ps 119:130 // Prov 8:5), *ṣedeq* 'righteousness' (Ps 119:7, 62, 75, 106, 121, 123, 138, 142, 144, 160, 164, 172 // Prov 8:8, 15, 16), *šmr* 'keep' (Ps 119:4, 5, 8, 9, 17, 34, 44, 55, 57, 60, 63, 67, 101, 106, 134, 136, 146, 158, 167, 168 // Prov 8:34), *šʿšʿ* 'delight' (Ps 119:16, 24, 47, 70, 77, 92, 143, 174 // Prov 8:30, 31).

who created them; yet each embodies an essential aspect of Yahweh that nevertheless can be addressed, invoked, and appealed to itself as the object of devotion. Each has the power to order and bless the worshiper's life.

The preeminent status of *tôrâ* in Psalm 119 can be judged by comparison with Psalm 19, widely regarded as a model for the former. Psalm 19 has 5 of the 8 key words (*tôrâ*, *ʿēdût* [singular], *miṣwâ* [singular], *piqqûdîm*, *mišpāṭîm*), and it makes statements about *tôrâ* that are practically identical to Psalm 119's. The crucial difference between the two psalms is the context for the celebration of *tôrâ*. Psalm 19 links *tôrâ* with Yahweh's power and revelation in creation, utilizing pre-Israelite solar imagery. *Tôrâ*, the psalm implies, is a manifestation of Yahweh's sovereignty, as is the natural world, the sun in particular. By contrast, in Psalm 119, despite occasional references to Yahweh's establishment of earth and heaven (vv. 89–90), creation as an analogy or counterpart of *tôrâ* has disappeared. The absence of creation as the context for *tôrâ* might be attributed in part to the difference in form between Psalms 19 and 119: laments, such as Psalm 119 (see below), the argument goes, contain fewer references to creation. But such an explanation cannot account for the almost complete lack of correlation between Yahweh's creation of the world and *tôrâ*. In Psalm 119, only Yahweh's *tôrâ* manifests Yahweh. *Tôrâ* is unique among Yahweh's creations.

Creation is not the only common Israelite theological concept missing in Psalm 119. Most importantly, the theology of Psalm 119 can be distinguished from Deuteronomic theology by what is left out of the psalm. Commentators have called the psalm Deuteronomic in thought, and there are certainly affinities between the psalm and Deuteronomy. Deuteronomy employs 7 of the key words (only *piqqûdîm* is absent), and many phrases appear in both places.[2] Most important, Psalm 119 employs the affective language of Deuteronomy: love (*ʾāhab*) of *tôrâ* with all one's heart, listening and keeping *tôrâ*. But *tôrâ* in Deuteronomy remains firmly grounded in Yahweh's mighty acts, as both the historical introduction and closing blessings and curses show. Psalm 119 has no trace of Deuteronomy's theological context for *tôrâ*. There is no mention of the Exodus or the promise of the land. Not even the covenant appears in Psalm 119. Compare Psalm 25, also an acrostic lament, which has *tôrâ* sentiments similar to Psalm 119's but explicitly links

2. Expressions in Psalm 119 also present in Weinfeld's catalog of Deuteronomic and Deuteronomistic phraseology (1992: 320–65) include *ʾāhab* 'love' (Ps 119:47, 48, 97, 113, 119, 127, 132, 159, 163, 165, 167), *bəkol-lēb* 'with a whole heart' (Ps 119:2, 10, 34, 58, 69, 145) and *hālak bĕtôrat yhwh* 'walk by Yahweh's *tôrâ*' (Ps 119:1). Also common to D and Psalm 119 is insistence on keeping (*šāmar*) to Yahweh's *derek* 'way' (see previous note) and to his *mišpāṭîm* 'laws' (Ps 119:7, 13, 20, 30, 39, 43, 52, 62, 75, 91, 102, 106, 108, 120, 137, 156, 164, 175).

tôrâ to covenant (25:10, 14). In Deuteronomy, *tôrâ* is a direct revelation of Yahweh. In Psalm 119, *tôrâ* is more: the perfect expression of Yahweh's nature and character, divorced from Israel's history, without Moses as mediator. *Tôrâ* is unique among Yahweh's mighty acts. Another major difference between Deuteronomic theology and Psalm 119 is the absence of the Deuteronomic "name theology" associated with the Temple. This is a paradox in Psalm 119, because *Tôra* itself (Genesis–Deuteronomy) has a great deal to say about the Temple (or Tabernacle), the sacrificial system, and Temple worship. Once again, this major part of Israelite religion has no representation in Psalm 119.

Psalm 119, then, has no explicit reference to the following Israelite theological ideas found elsewhere throughout the Hebrew Bible: creation; patriarchal promises; covenants (patriarchal, Mosaic, or Davidic); the Temple; the Davidic dynasty, past or future; or Yahweh's mighty acts of salvation in Israel's history. Only *tôrâ* is left as the theological category of Yahweh's revelation and activity in the world. Does this mean that the psalmist has rejected the ideas and concepts omitted from the psalm? Not if, as common sense would dictate, the *tôrâ* that the psalm exalts includes at least the Pentateuch. The totality of *tôrâ* is perfect. Whether narrative or law, prose or poetry—not one verse is superfluous; this is the message of the acrostic form. The synonyms for *tôrâ*, which with the word *tôrâ* comprise the 8 key words, show however, that in Psalm 119 the essence of *tôrâ* is Yahweh's revelation of his teaching: the precepts, commandments, laws, words, stipulations, and pronouncements. Everything else in Israelite religion—Temple, Covenant, Creation, Exodus, Messiah—is subsumed under *tôrâ* defined according to the 7 synonyms.

The 8 *tôrâ*-words provide the inner logic of the poem's message of the inexhaustibility of *tôrâ*, just as the eightfold acrostic structure provides the outer form. As shown in the preceding essays, the psalmist uses the 8 words more or less interchangeably. The other 7 words are essentially synonyms for *tôrâ*. Since *tôrâ* is the *summum bonum*, not only of the psalmist's life but also of the whole Bible, it appears more frequently than any other key word (25 times). Its synonyms serve to elaborate and vary the poem's essential message without changing its meaning. Some commentators (e.g., Briggs 1909: 415) have attempted to attach specific nuances to each key word. The psalm's message, however, derives not from use of particular words in single verses but from the complex interplay of the 8 key words throughout the psalm.

Thus *tôrâ* in Psalm 119 has two meanings. First, it is the sacred, authoritative, written revelation of God. The psalm leaves ambiguous the exact identity of this sacred text. It may be an unknown collection of protopentateuchal texts. It may be the Pentateuch, which Ezra edited and brought back to Jerusalem as the nation's charter (Nehemiah 8). It may be the Primary History or even the entire Hebrew Bible essentially as it exists today (minus Daniel). Whatever its identity, *tôrâ* is the definitive sacred text. Second, *tôrâ*, as the other key words delimit it, is the specific revelation of God's will in the various instructions that the sacred text contains. The psalm's omission of so much of Israelite history and theology, then, does not imply rejection of existing traditions. Rather, those traditions function only to explain, support, or exalt Yahweh's unique, unparalleled revelation, the purpose of all Yahweh's dealings with Israel: *tôrâ*.

Deducing a Sitz im Leben for almost any psalm is difficult. Due to its single-minded focus on the *tôrat-yhwh*, Psalm 119 presents a paucity of clues concerning the date and purpose of its composition. One can say, however, that its exaltation of *tôrâ* suggests a corresponding decline in the other main Israelite religious ideas discussed above. Yahweh's mighty acts for the nation are not mythological; presumably they're part of *tôrâ*, the sacred text. But they are ancient history, and the psalm ignores the possibility that Yahweh would act definitively again. Yahweh's definitive act is simply *tôrâ*. Yahweh's covenant consists of the gift of *tôrâ*, whether Israel occupies the land or languishes in exile. Even the Temple, the center of Israelite worship, is just a by-product of *tôrâ*. What matters is not meticulous observance of Temple protocols, though they are important to priests, according to *tôrâ*. What matters is meticulous exploration of *tôrâ* itself. Such exploration can be done by priest and nonpriest alike, in any place, not just Jerusalem. All of these considerations suggest a time in Israel's history when *tôrâ* has become, or is on its way to becoming, the heart and soul of the Israelite community. The author may be part of a vanguard of *tôrâ*-centered Israelites. Or the author may express a dominant, official ideology. In any case, a plausible time period for this psalm is the rule of Ezra or Nehemiah, each of whom sought to make *tôrâ* the ruling document for the restored Jerusalem.

Psalm 119 is constructed so as to repay the closest attention. This is deliberate, for it expresses the psalmist's deepest conviction: the *tôrat yhwh* repays the closest attention. The neophyte can read the essence of the psalm in v. 1, just as one can read all of *tôrâ* in the Decalogue. But the psalm also contains treasures of subtlety and brilliance that require repeated investigation to uncover; so it is with *tôrâ* to the highest degree, for only *tôrâ* reveals Yahweh.

Form and Content

Psalm 119 hymns the majesty, sublimity, and perfection of *tôrâ*. But the poem's employment of the 8 key words reinforces another theme of the psalm as well. As noted above, several commentators have been bothered by the lack of one-to-one correspondence between lines and key words and have emended the text to produce a better, that is, more straightforward and comprehensible, organization. In the actual psalm, however, there is no such simple, reliable use of the key words: subtotals of key words vary from stanza to stanza; key words are missing from some verses and doubled in others. The perfection of the *tôrat yhwh* is not reflected in an unvarying model of 1 key word per verse, 8 key words per stanza. Unlike Genesis 1, with its magisterial unfolding of God's sovereignty, Psalm 119's structure, though ruled on one hand by the rigid acrostic pattern and on the other by *tôrâ* and its synonyms, is on first inspection bewildering and unpredictable. The poet's art in intertwining the key words—their numbers, position, and pairing—appears simply chaotic.

The two poles of the poem's framework, then, are order (the acrostic format) and (apparent) chaos (the distribution of key words). These two poles are precisely reflected in the psalm's content: the totality of the psalm proclaims the perfection of *tôrâ*, but the psalm's verses and stanzas reflect a life of chaos, trouble, and ambiguity. Soll (1991: chap. 3) has shown persuasively that the psalm is an individual lament. Ninety verses of the psalm—over one-half—are petitions for Yahweh's mercy, compassion, or salvation. The psalmist is surrounded and harassed by enemies (*ṣārîm*, vv. 139, 157; *ʾōyĕbay*, v. 98), be they princes (*śārîm*, vv. 23, 161), the arrogant (*zēdîm*, vv. 21, 51, 69, 78, 85, 122), the wicked (*rĕšāʿîm*, vv. 53, 61, 95, 110, 155), oppressors (*ʿōšĕqay*, vv. 121, 134), or persecutors (*rōdĕpay*, vv. 84, 150, 157). Dedication to the *tôrat-yhwh* has created powerful opposition.

Nor does Yahweh automatically reward the psalmist's devotion. In numerous phrases, many of them identical to phrases found in other psalms, the psalmist describes his wretched life and calls upon Yahweh not to abandon him. In the end, the psalmist has only *tôrâ* itself to sustain him (see especially the *kap* stanza, vv. 81–88).

The psalm's content, then, is founded on the stark contrast between the psalmist's exaltation of *tôrâ* (Yahweh's complete and perfect revelation) and his own humiliation (the chaos of his life). The first and last verses provide a compelling example of this contrast. V. 1 celebrates the blameless way, the *tôrat-yhwh*, and announces blessing to those who follow it. V. 176 portrays the psalmist as "wandering like a lost sheep," calling upon Yahweh for safety and salvation.

This analysis leads to one fundamental conclusion: there is a direct correspondence between the structure and content of Psalm 119. Order is represented structurally by the psalm's acrostic form and 8 key words, substantively by the psalm's encomia upon *tôrâ*. Chaos appears in the convolutions of the application of the 8 key words, paralleled by the psalmist's own situation. Not only has the psalmist composed the most elaborate and intricate psalm in the Psalter, he has also taken exquisite care to create a precise congruity between its configuration and its contents.

The tension between order and chaos is an essential feature of the psalm, but order and chaos are not equal forces. As mathematicians have demonstrated in chaos theory, chaos is not the same as randomness; chaos can be quantified and described. In Psalm 119, the 8 key words appear in identifiable patterns, not randomly (see chaps. 2–3 above). Thus even the psalm's fine details are ordered, and the apparent chaos of the key words is ultimately resolved. Theologically, there is no doubt that Yahweh's *tôrâ* reigns supreme in this psalm.

The data presented here open new avenues of investigation of Psalm 119. There is much more work to be done, both on the compositional complexities of the psalm itself and on the interplay between form and content. In particular, the discernment of an overarching thematic plan in the psalm has occupied many scholars. Another major question still unsolved is the psalm's setting and the identity of its speaker. Is this a royal psalm, written for an actual king in the seventh century (Dahood 1970: 173) or in exile (Soll 1991: 152–54), or an ideal Deuteronomic king (Soll 1991: 126)? This issue may be indeterminable, but one certainty remains: like *tôrâ* for the psalmist, Psalm 119 deserves the most serious study.[3]

3. We thank Miriam Sherman for her assistance in the preparation of this chapter.

Bibliography

Alter, R.
1985 *The Art of Biblical Poetry.* New York: Basic Books.

Briggs, C. A., and Briggs, E. G.
1909 *Psalms.* ICC. New York: Scribner's.

Buttenwieser, M.
1969 *The Psalms.* The Library of Biblical Studies. New York: KTAV.

Dahood, M.
1970 *Psalms 101–150.* AB 17A. Garden City, New York: Doubleday.

Kraus, H. J.
1989 *Psalms 60–150.* Minneapolis: Augsburg.

Oesterley, W. O. E.
1955 *The Psalms.* London: SPCK.

Soll, W.
1991 *Psalm 119: Matrix, Form and Setting.* CBQMS 23. Washington, D.C.: Catholic Biblical Association of America.

Weiser, A.
1962 *The Psalms.* OTL. Philadelphia: Westminster.

Weinfeld, M.
1992 *Deuteronomy and the Deuteronomic School.* Oxford: Oxford University Press, 1972. Reprinted Winona Lake, Indiana: Eisenbrauns.